ONCE YOU WERE NO PEOPLE

**ONCE YOU WERE NO PEOPLE
BUT NOW YOU ARE GOD'S PEOPLE.**
— 1 Peter 2:10 —

ONCE YOU WERE NO PEOPLE
THE CHURCH AND THE TRANSFORMATION OF SOCIETY

T. RICHARD SNYDER

MEYER STONE BOOKS

© 1988 by T. Richard Snyder

All rights reserved. No part of this book may be reproduced in any manner whatsoever without written permission of the publisher, except brief quotations embodied in critical articles or reviews.

Published in the United States by Meyer-Stone Books,
a division of Meyer, Stone, and Company, Inc.,
2014 South Yost Avenue, Bloomington, IN 47403

Cover design: Terry Dugan Design

Manufactured in the United States of America
92   5 4 3

Typesetting output: TEXSource, Houston

Library of Congress Cataloging in Publication Data

Snyder, T. Richard, 1936–
   Once you were no people.

   Bibliography: p.
   1. Alienation (Theology)   2. Reconciliation —
Religious aspects — Christianity.   I. Title.
BT731.053   1988   233'.5   87-42728
ISBN 0-940989-25-5

To my father,
Theodore F. Snyder,
April 7, 1907–December 18, 1984,
one of God's People

Contents

Acknowledgments   xi

Preface   xiii

PART ONE
"Driven from the Garden":
The Reality of Our Alienation
Page 1

1   **"Once You Were No People":**
     The Forms of Our Alienation   3

     The Other as Threat: Alienation from Our Neighbor   6
     The Job as Grindstone: Alienation from Our Work   8
     Nature as Commodity:
        Alienation from Our Environment   10
     You Can't Fight City Hall:
        Alienation from Our Institutions   11
     Cracked Mirrors: Alienation from Ourselves   13
     A Great Chasm Is Fixed: Alienation from God   14

2   **"Bricks without Straw":**
     The Mechanisms of Our Alienation   16

     Imposed Identities: The Implication of Inferiority   16
     Imposed Relations: The Structures of Alienation   24

3	**"Scattered over the Face of the Earth": False Responses to Alienation**	**31**
	Resignation to Fate	*33*
	Denying the Problem	*40*
	Blaming the Victim	*43*
	Keeping Busy	*47*
	Hope in Magic	*50*

PART TWO
"From No People to God's People": The Process of Transformation
Page 55

4	**"Woe Is Me": The Recognition of Incoherence**	**58**
	Sin	*64*
	Christology	*65*
	Eschatology	*66*
	Preaching as Truth-Telling	*68*
	Prayer as Groaning	*70*
	Counselling as Unveiling	*72*
5	**"Where There Is No Vision the People Perish": Imagining the Future**	**75**
	Revelation and Vision	*80*
	Space and Vision	*81*
	Vision and Play	*82*
	Play and the Sacraments	*83*
	Vision and Meditation	*86*
	Meditation and the Word	*86*

6	**"Crucified, Dead, and Buried":** **Conflict as the Mid-Wife of the Future**	**91**
	Conflict and the Doctrine of the Atonement	*96*
	Eucharist as the Taste of Death	*101*
	Preaching as Conflict	*104*
7	**"New Wineskins for New Wine":** **Institutionalizing the Vision**	**107**
	Parabolic Actions	*112*
	Sects	*114*
	Revolutions	*116*
	Establishments	*118*

Epilogue: "Thy Kingdom Come":
Perfection or Approximation?   **127**

    The Vision of God's Reign   *131*
    The Historical Project   *132*

Notes   **137**

Acknowledgments

In a certain sense, this book has been twenty years in the brewing. Its ingredients come from a myriad of sources too numerous to mention. Traditionally, footnotes have been the approved academic way in which to acknowledge one's indebtedness, so I've included some in order to indicate, in part, the important influences on my thinking. However, the ingredients provided by the communities and persons with whom I have been engaged over the years in trying to figure out what it means to be faithful to the gospel today have been of inestimable importance. To acknowledge all of them adequately would require a separate book. So I take the risk of gross abbreviation in recognizing those who have been so important to me in bringing the book to fruition.

I wish to thank my colleagues, the board, and the students at New York Theological Seminary. This book was primarily written during a sabbatical leave for which I am most grateful. But most of all, I wish to thank them for being the most exciting theological education community that I know of that works on issues of transformation. My colleagues have supported and loved me, my students have stimulated and challenged me, and together we have sought to bring about transformation in our metropolis.

It all began long before I arrived at New York Theological Seminary, of course. Dick Shaull, my Ph.D. advisor at Princeton, was and has continued to be a shaping influence in my thinking. The staff of Metropolitan Associates of Philadelphia, long since dispersed, was instrumental in discussing and testing some of its early form. The staff and students of ISTEM, an urban theological consortium program, fed my thinking a great deal. The faithful folks with whom I worked in an ad hoc, low-income housing coalition in Jersey City, which has now emerged as the newly formed Interfaith Community Organization, have provided something of a base community for me for a number of years.

I want especially to mention my gratitude to Robert McAfee Brown for his painstaking reading of the first draft, for his suggestions, and his encouragement. What he did was a labor of love. I also wish to thank my colleague, Norman Gottwald, who read the manuscript and was a source of constant encouragement.

No one likes to be corrected, of course, and to be corrected by one's spouse is doubly difficult. It has been suggested that for a spouse to edit one's work is to flirt with divorce. I should like to report that we have survived, indeed, thrived. My wife, Carole, has read and re-read, edited, discussed substance, argued, and helped in every aspect of the writing. I am deeply grateful.

Lastly, I wish to acknowledge the people who struggle against all odds to survive and those who are engaged in the struggle for transformation. Many of them know nothing of me. But I have been moved and shaped by their lives and their struggle.

Preface

It is strange how events turn our lives unexpectedly. This year I am fifty. Nothing in the early part of my life would have led me to expect that I would have the kinds of concerns, perspective, and commitments that I have today. It's not even that I want to be where I am; it is rather that something has caught me and won't let go.

The shattering of my protected world began with a seminary internship in Rio de Janeiro, Brazil, in 1961–62. As the assistant minister of the English-speaking Union Church I was provided luxurious accommodations of which I had only dared to dream. Living in the homes of vacationing U.S. business executives in an economy where services were cheap, I enjoyed servants, chauffeurs, cooks, and swimming pools. The president of Brazil lived directly above "my" apartment on Copocabana beach.

A stone's throw from this luxury were the *favelas,* the tin-and-cardboard shanty towns in which refugees from rural poverty gathered in the empty dream that the city might offer a new life. They had nothing to go back to, but they had nothing in the *favelas* either: no running water, no schools, no police protection, no sewage system, no hope. The contrast shook me to the core.

I thought I was leaving all this behind when I made a leisurely trip home through Peru and Mexico. I was wrong. Wherever I went it was the same. Tens of thousands of impoverished rural migrants were living in squalid urban conditions without hope, side-by-side with ostentatious luxury. Beggars juxtaposed with Mercedes became the symbol of Latin America for me.

Back in the States, the Civil Rights movement was beginning to unveil the same discrepancies. A society that enjoyed enormous wealth and privileges was revealed as having a wretched underside; an entire people deprived of their basic rights, a decent living, dignity, and freedom because of their color. Many of us began to speak to people with whom we had never spoken, visit areas where we had never gone, and discover painful truths we had not known.

More and more voices have been added to those of the Latin American poor and U.S. blacks — the elderly who have been forgotten and discarded, the children of war, the women who have been abused and controlled, the gays and lesbians who have been denied their rights, the homeless who have nowhere to go. And it goes on. As the stridency of these voices increased, many of us responded with fear and guilt: fear that the demands would deprive us of what we have enjoyed, and guilt in recognition that many of our privileges were being purchased at others' expense. Both of these responses led to a dead end. The fear led to resistance and the guilt to immobilization.

Gradually I have come to understand that the problem is not just someone else's. What has become increasingly clear to me is that none of us is exempt from the experience of being used, being marginal, being insecure, being despised, being cut off. It is different for each of us, but it is also the same. It is not "them against us." It is our common calamity. Only as we come to understand how we share in the tragedy of a world so divided by injustice and hostility is there any hope for reconciliation. Anything less may deal with the plight of a few, but at stake is the redemption of all of humanity.

This book is an attempt to move beyond recrimination and resistance, beyond allegation and denial, to understand the alienation in which we all share, and to point to some directions that offer hope. It is about alienation because that is our condition. It is also about resurrection, because that is our hope — a hope that in the face of alienation, reconciliation is possible.

This may not appear, at first, to be a book about hope. If one were to read only the first section, confidence in creation's goodness and the power of redemption might not be evident. That is because the book begins by looking at the alienation in which we so frequently are caught. It is not because I am a pessimist that I begin this way, but because there is no point considering transformation until we have first understood what needs to be changed. Our alienation is not the whole picture, but it is what we must look at first.

Part One begins with our alienation: the forms it takes, the mechanisms by which it is created and sustained, and the false responses that only exacerbate the problem. In particular, it explores the ways in which the churches often unwittingly contribute to false responses through their teachings, liturgies, and pastoral activities. That is not the whole story, but it is unfortunately often the case. Until we adequately understand what we are up against, we may find that our attempts to solve things only make matters worse. The cure may kill the patient.

Part Two attempts to delineate the stages in a process of transformation: awakening, envisioning, conflict, and rebuilding. This approach weaves together my experiences, the witness of Scripture, and some contemporary theories about how fundamental change occurs. While there is little offered that will further the theoretical discussion, what is new, and I trust helpful, is the attempt to show how doctrines, liturgical practices, and pastoral activities are, and can be, a vital part of the process of transformation for those who are rooted in the Christian community. It is my conviction that the churches have frequently been a fundamental part of the problem, but I believe that is neither the desire of our God nor a necessity.

If we claim to be a resurrection people, a people of God's Reign, then it is essential that we seek to understand the forces of death, sickness, and alienation that abound in our world and to combat them at every turn.

Alienation is not a mere problem to be solved. It is a tragedy of immense proportions. Transformation, the conversion from alienation to reconciliation, is what God is about in Jesus Christ. It is the calling that we have received. We who were once "No People" have been transformed for the sake of the transformation of the cosmos that groans and travails. Transformation of our world is the will of God, but it cannot be accomplished by God alone. It is our calling and our role that this book is about.

PART ONE

"Driven from the Garden": The Reality of Our Alienation

ACCORDING TO THE BOOK OF GENESIS, it all begins in the Garden. The Fall of Adam and Eve set humans ever afterward on a journey away from God, the environment, work, each other, and their true selves. But this ancient story has a power far beyond its time because it is our story as well. It captures the universal and all-encompassing nature of the alienation we experience. We are an alienated people who live in the midst of an alienated world.

Alienation is the process of being made foreign or estranged, of being cut off. The term, as it is used here, assumes that we are made foreign to what is rightfully ours, as in the experience of exile, enslavement, or exploitation. To be alienated is to be severed from one's proper place, rightful condition, and appropriate relationships. Just as the biblical narrative begins by facing human alienation, so, too, must our story. Until we uncover the origins and reality of our alienation there is no possibility for transformation.

The three chapters of Part One set forth an understanding of the nature of our alienation: first, its contemporary forms, second, the mechanisms of its perpetuation, and third, some false responses that only deepen the problem.

Chapter 1

"Once You Were No People": The Forms of Our Alienation

Juan and María came to the United States from Central America as young adults, sneaking into the country after a tortuous journey that began with their escape from a political dictatorship that was seeking to imprison them for peaceful protest against their government. They must pretend to be Puerto Rican in order to pass for United States citizens and not be deported. They are "illegal aliens" who cannot use their own names for fear of discovery. They live with their two children in a shabby, one-bedroom, fourth-floor walk-up apartment. They work "off the books" with no official record of their work submitted to Internal Revenue, Social Security, the city, or the state. They are paid less than minimum wage but are afraid to complain lest their employer report them to Immigration. Their lives are in jeopardy economically, politically, and culturally. They are among the lost people of our world.

The Gentile Christians of the early church who lived in Asia Minor were like Juan and María. They, too, knew what it meant to be a people without security or rights. They were scattered among the towns and cities and were a despised and insecure people. They lacked the protection afforded Roman citizens and were no longer part of the recognized Jewish religion of which Christianity was originally considered a sect. They therefore no longer enjoyed the minimal toleration given to the Jews. In many respects their lives were like those of today's political and economic exiles. To those "nobodies" the author of 1 Peter wrote these words of hope: "Once you were no people, but now you are God's people." They knew that he was referring to the "No People" who had suffered under slavery in Egypt, living in a land not their own, without dignity, self-direction, or hope. But those "No People" had been made special by God. They had been called out of darkness to shine as a light to the nations. The early Christians knew both from their own lives and from the narrative of the Exodus what it meant to be a nobody.

Being a nobody — without true name and without a place to stand — is our condition as well. At first glance this may not be entirely evident. It was not always so to me. Such a bleak assessment of my condition seemed unreal as a young white man growing up in the protective environment of the suburbs with its promise of unending upward mobility for the diligent and gifted. Tennessee Williams and Arthur Miller's harsh depictions of life not only seemed remote but fabricated by incredibly perverse minds. While our church taught that all had sinned and come short of the glory of God, it was impossible to believe that life was filled with such failure and destructiveness. I did not believe that we, nor many others, were in the dreadful condition of being "no people." I was special and I knew it. Though I mouthed the words of the hymn "to such as worm as I" and was filled with guilt for the most menial of oversights, it never dawned on me that the world was filled with persons who had no place, no name, no rights, no chance of survival. Least of all it never occurred to me that my own condition might be of that sort.

Arthur Miller's *Death of a Salesman* appalled me as a college student.[1] Defeat and tragedy seemed exaggerated for the sake of sensationalism. I have seen the play again recently and am now convinced that Miller has captured some of the most essential aspects of life in Western society.

Willie Loman, a sixty-three-year-old man, after years of trying to be a successful salesman, is without a job, without purpose, without money, without intimacy, and without hope. To make up for all he lacks he resorts to delusion ("I averaged $170 a week in sales then"), illusion ("It's not what you say, it's how you say it"), buying affection with gifts, and denial. He pretends that life is brighter than its stark reality, that his son is not a thief and a drifter, and that even though he can no longer get appointments he is well known and respected in his old territory. He is a tragic figure, alienated from all around him and most especially from his true self.

To me, Willie epitomizes much of Western society. We are a society of salespeople. Our selling goes far beyond the traditional arena of merchandising products to include almost every endeavor of life. The "professionalization" of our world has come about as a response to a system that seeks profit above all else, and consequently almost everything is for sale. Even the traditional helping professions of medicine, law, and ministry have succumbed.

The *Wall Street Journal* reported that the median professional earnings (which does not include investment income) for an office-based physician in 1984 were nearly $102,000.[2] A Canadian-trained physician confided to me that had he been born in the United States rather than in Canada he might have become a minister. In Canada when he was training, medicine was a calling. In the United States it is an entrepreneurial field. It is small wonder that the majority of general practitioners and specialists are to be found in the affluent areas while the poorer inner cities and rural areas are desperately underserved. The doctors are simply going where the money is.

Many in the legal profession receive similarly inflated salaries in service to corporations and wealthy individuals. While there is a dearth of lawyers available to serve the poor, there is a glut on the market in other areas. Nonetheless, the graduates of the prestigious law schools are being sought assiduously and being paid starting salaries in excess of $60,000 a year.

While it may be clear that a majority of doctors and lawyers have opted for selling, over healing and helping, it is also increasingly true of the clergy. Television is filled with Sunday morning hucksters, and successful churches are defined as those with ever increasing membership and large budgets. Far too many sermons seem based on Willie Loman's adage, "It's not what you say but how you say it that counts." They package Jesus Christ and Christianity like a product or service competing in the open market. The Church Growth movement, to cite an example, emphasizes size at the expense of inclusiveness, risk-taking, and social justice.[3] The blunt reality, however, is that most of our churches are small and struggling to survive. Try as we may to live up to the myths and promises of a sales-oriented world, we are failing.

Even in the church many of us, like Willie Loman, are living with false illusions about our lives that enable us to escape the realization that we are cut off from all that is around us and from our true selves. In a word, we are an alienated people and dwell in the midst of an alienated world.

If this seems too harsh a judgment about life in our society, remember that the claim of fundamental alienation as the human condition is not new. It is pictured in the stories of the Fall and the Tower of Babel, in Paul's theology of a world groaning for salvation, in Augustine's claim that "thou hast made us for ourselves and our hearts are restless until they find their rest in thee," in Calvin's notion of Total Depravity, and in Barth's doctrine of God who is "totally other." It is a central picture of human experience offered us by both the Hebrew and Christian Scriptures and most of Christian tradition.

All is not negative, of course. There is beauty and goodness in the creation, grace and love characterize many a relationship, and moments of sheer delight are often ours. It is the contrast that serves to make the alienation so painful to admit openly.

Just as Miller's tragic figure of Willie Loman seemed so removed from reality to me as a youth, most people today find it either too painful or too preposterous to face their condition. Society conspires to hide the painful truth and to offer illusory promises that anesthetize us to our true feelings.[4] But no matter how dulled our perception, in the quiet moments we know that our world is alienated and alienating. Its forms are varied but the alienation affects every aspect of our lives.

The Other as Threat: Alienation from Our Neighbor

Perhaps the most obvious form of alienation we experience is the dividing wall of hostility that has risen up among us. In Jersey City, where my family and I live, many Hispanics are being driven from their homes by the gentrifiers, most of whom are white. Blacks and Hispanics within our city are fighting for the same crumbs. Whites with whom I talk routinely perceive people of color as thieves, muggers, and destroyers of the peace and beauty of the neighborhood. Many of the younger adults see the elderly residents who have been there for forty and fifty years as a drag on the momentum for change. The old feel neglected and forgotten. The poor view the rich with contempt or envy, while the rich tend to distinguish between the honest poor for whom they feel pity and the "no-goods" whom they disdain.

Jersey City is not unique. In Philadelphia, New York, Rio de Janeiro, the suburbs of Pennsylvania and New Jersey, and coastal Maine where I have lived, the reality is the same though the specifics are different. As Ephesians says, there is a dividing wall of hostility and it is as real as any concrete or brick structure.

Sometimes it is subtle, hardly what you'd recognize as alienation between people. But it is there. One evening in a suburb of Philadelphia I gathered with seven salesmen who wanted to explore the relationship between their faith and their work. Predictable platitudes gave way to agonizing revelations as one after another of the men related how their entire lives were shaped by the competitiveness of their work. They divided the world into customers, potential customers, or competitors for the customers. For them, the problem arose when they went home and tried to relate to their families in non-competitive ways. At the very best, they felt themselves schizophrenic; at the worst, they were unable to make the shift between work and home.

Sometimes it is inescapable, hanging heavily over us. In Jersey City you can feel the hostility as you walk the streets, attend city council meetings, or gather at a neighbor's house for a social time. Animosities run high, exacerbated in our case by the former mayor who alternately denied the existence of racial tensions, problems of displacement, and homelessness and then blamed the problems on the poor. His attitude, unusual only in its candor, was epitomized in a private conversation among four of us at a library benefit. Discussing a proposed supermarket in our downtown area, one individual expressed concern about the amount of filth that would attend its presence. The mayor's response was, "The filth is already here. It is living in the Section Eight houses that the liberals put up." The one who had initiated the topic told the mayor that by filth he had in mind pollution from the traffic and litter. But by then the mayor had shown his hand.

In the June 1985 Democratic primary, which is tantamount

to election in Jersey City, the mayor was soundly defeated, largely by those very people whom he considered filth. The stunning and unexpected upset revealed the depth of the divisions that exist in our city. The mayor was simply a lightning rod for an already alienated community.

No, our city is not alone. The divisions between blacks and whites, Anglos and Hispanics, young and old, rich and poor, Jews and Gentiles, Protestants and Catholics, longtime residents and newcomers, are as American as apple pie. The myth of the melting pot is at best a pipe dream and at worst a fabrication to serve the interests of those in control.

These divisions are not confined to our cities or even our own nation. They extend to our nationalisms, the cold war between East and West, and the severe economic disparities between the northern and southern hemispheres. These divisions, which most of us experience only on a small scale, have culminated in the gross alienations of slavery, the Holocaust, and apartheid.

While there are pockets of friendship that cross these lines, they are the exception rather than the rule. We are a people who stand in relation to each other as threat.

The Job as Grindstone: Alienation from Our Work

With few exceptions, most of us sell our labor. It is all we have to sell. This is abundantly clear in the case of the factory worker or the service person but less clear for professionals and managers. Those of us who manage others or who have some degree of control over our schedule usually don't think of ourselves as selling our labor. But the reality of most of us is that we are salaried employees who are dependent upon those salaries both for our style of life and our survival. We have nothing to barter except our labor and our skills, and we must sell them to those who own the basic resources and organizations of our society.

For most of us, work is a necessary evil, aptly captured by the aphorisms that one is "a cog in a machine" or we must "keep our nose to the grindstone." While many of the horrendous conditions of early industrialism, such as child labor, twelve-hour days, and sweat shops, have been eliminated for most people through the organized efforts of the labor movement, the fact remains that the majority have nothing to sell but their labor. Consequently some of the most basic negative dynamics of that period still pertain.

People have little or no say over the product of their labor and hence derive little or no satisfaction from their work. The function of work for the majority is not to create something that can give a sense of accomplishment, but to earn money to survive and do a few enjoyable things. If we compare our experience of work with the Genesis account of the creation, the contrast is startling. God conceived, God acted, God created, and God saw that it was good. And then on the seventh day God rested, the rest of one who knows satisfaction with one's work. In our jobs most of us are not allowed to follow the process of conception, action, and creation; we do not see the fruits of our labor, or know true rest. Our work is initiated by others, the product seldom seen by us, and the rest we do get is that of exhaustion. Thus we are twice drained, once from the physical exertion, once from the psychic dissatisfaction.

For Karl Marx, all alienation — from others, from ourselves, from our world — emanates from the relationship of the worker to the means of production. It is because the ownership and control of the means of production reside in the hands of a few privileged people that the majority of human beings are reduced to a state of fundamental alienation. All other forms of alienation are outcomes of this fundamental cause.[5]

It is a mistake, however, to think that Marx reduced all of life to economics or that he did not recognize many other aspects of life as giving shape to our world. He is, at best, quite inclusive in his understanding, and, at worst, ambiguous. Certainly in his earlier works he is clear about the numerous factors that impact our lives. Many contemporary Marxists have emphasized the critical role of culture, including religion, in the dynamic of alienation and its elimination.[6] What Marx insists is that we cannot understand alienation unless we understand its economic roots. Certainly we can see something of the logic of this analysis when we note the linkage between various forms of abuse (of substances, or of people) among the poor. In fact, there is a predictable rise in crime with each increment in unemployment. The critical factor here is not income but lack of control over one's life that results in rage and destructive behavior. Whether or not one uses Marxist analysis to understand the nature of work and its consequences for us, it is undeniable that for most of us work is a form of alienation.

Nature as Commodity: Alienation from Our Environment

Within the last fifty years alone, advances in communication, in travel, and in medicine have probably outstripped all combined human invention in the prior history of humankind. But this has often been at great cost both in terms of immediate consequences for people's lives (such as those at Hiroshima) and in terms of the more subtle shift in our relation to nature in general (such as the increase in pollution). Much of science and technology approach nature as an object to be manipulated. By setting the limits according to what is achievable rather than what is desirable, we have desecrated the earth and developed the potential to eliminate all human life.

Those of us who live in urban environments experience enormous alienation from nature. We breathe air filled with toxic poisons, necessitating some to remain indoors for entire days. Residents of rural New England discover lakes once abundantly filled with fish now empty from the results of acid rain. Pesticides have become so lethal that entire crops have had to be destroyed to prevent humans from consuming them. The rape (called development) of the Amazon River basin threatens to upset the world's basic oxygen supply since almost one quarter of our oxygen is produced from the vegetation in that area. A chemical leak at the Union Carbide plant in Bhopal, India, killed thousands and maimed or caused serious sickness in tens of thousands. Nuclear accidents such as Three Mile Island and Chernobyl have brought fear and disruption to the lives of all those living near a nuclear plant. Toxic poisons buried under Love Canal forced the entire community to be moved. Military chemicals such as Agent Orange have destroyed our own troops as well as "the enemy." And finally, in what may be our ultimate folly, we have created and continue to manufacture a nuclear arms supply capable of erasing all life from the face of the earth.

In our mad race to dominate our environment we have dramatically increased our own disease, fear, and potential for death. Perhaps at no other time in history have a people been so alienated from their environment.

But our alienation does not end there. It cuts to the very roots of our style of being in the world. Many of us have become so enamored with the control and manipulation of nature that we no longer are able to relate to the environment. Our dependence upon the automobile has cut us off from the beauty of a flower discovered. Our hermetically sealed offices have removed us from the flow of weather. We have lost the ability to wonder, to be awestruck by nature: more enamored of an airplane than a bird, the noise of a digital recording than the sound of the cricket, more struck by the beauty of steel and glass than of a simple tree.

It is not that we should forgo our appreciation of the beauties of technological creation. It is neither possible nor desirable to seek a return to more primitive times. Rather, it is that in treating nature primarily as a thing to be used we are losing our capacity to be fully in touch with the totality of our environment. We are alienated from that which surrounds us and of which we are a part.

You Can't Fight City Hall: Alienation from Our Institutions

Most of the institutions created to serve us no longer do so — if they ever did. I took a Hispanic friend who was suffering from severe abdominal pain to a New York hospital emergency room. We waited there for three hours before seeing a doctor. During that time, as scores jammed the waiting room, we and others were treated with bureaucratic coldness, misinformation, and evasion. Frightened patients and families were herded like cattle. When it was finally our turn, my friend received perfunctory medical treatment. The tragedy of the situation is that this occurred in the emergency room of a church-founded hospital staffed predominantly by blacks and Hispanics who themselves had experienced the same kind of inhumane treatment throughout their lives. If one were to expect humane health care, why not here? The other tragedy is that such treatment is no aberration. Many can repeat such horror stories themselves.

As most of us know, the institutions that have been created by us to serve us — health care, transportation, energy, communications, education — have run amuck. Except for the few, they fail to achieve their intended purposes, in many cases actually making life more inhumane.

Our health care system is a misnomer. It is geared to profit-making for the rulers of the medical industry. It is neither healthful nor caring. Little if any focus is given to preventive care; rather, massive funds and energies are applied to esoteric research and experimentation. Further, the limited primary care that is available is uneven, and if one is poor it is provided under the most restricted and demeaning of circumstances. Those of us who have had any connection with the American Health Empire find it to be no surprise that our nation falls behind many poorer countries, including Cuba, in the provision of basic health care.[7]

Our educational system has been a failure as well. In some areas of New York City one can expect as few as 20 percent of the incoming freshmen to graduate from high school. Adult illiteracy is a national scandal. Jonathan Kozol estimates that over 20 percent of all adults in the United States are functionally illiterate, unable to read simple instructions.[8] An institution designed to enable persons to become mature, articulate, critical thinkers has too frequently produced mindless followers.

Teaching, which used to be a highly respected profession, has fallen to second-class status. Low pay, along with decreasing prestige and untenable working conditions, have taken their toll. In some areas of New York City police are regularly present in the halls and even intermittently in the classrooms to prevent physical violence. Dedicated teachers, administrators, and students frequently find it difficult, if not impossible, to get on with the business of education.

Some of our mass transit systems, designed to move us about safely, swiftly, and economically, have become a shambles. Those of us who ride the subways in the metropolitan New York area know the experience of being crammed into filthy, overheated, unsafe, often delayed, crime-ridden cars. The inhumanity of the experience and its toll on the quality of the life of its riders can hardly be exaggerated. Instead of being transported, we emerge from the transit facility feeling violated. In many rural areas such as Maine the problem is not overcrowding but lack of any mass transit at all. Counties that were once served by trains and buses now lack any public service, forcing some of the poorest people in our country to rely on costly automobile transport.

We could go on, but there is no need. The fact is that for most of us the very institutions that have been designed to serve our needs have turned on us like malevolent Leviathans, devouring our humanity and further alienating us from life.

Cracked Mirrors: Alienation from Ourselves

When I was forty years old a friend asked me about my own suffering. My response was quick and unequivocal. "I have not known suffering first-hand." Such a statement might seem possible for a white, middle-class male growing up in the United States but, in fact, it was a lie — or rather a delusion. Somehow I had managed to block the humiliation I felt for my father who, as a blue-collar worker, was treated without dignity and who expressed his rage at home. Somehow I had managed to block the loss and dread I experienced when blinded in one eye at age twelve. Somehow I had managed to ignore the pain of a failed marriage. Somehow I had managed to forget the desperation that one night led me to consider suicide.

Being out of touch with ourselves constitutes life for so many. It is as if we were gazing into a broken mirror, making it impossible for us to recognize the truth about ourselves. We have closed ourselves off from our feelings, our aspirations, our true selves. We have become so busy playing the roles assigned to us that we no longer know who we really are. Like Willie Loman, our identities have become confused, borrowed from a textbook that prescribes who we should be. We are what we do. We have confused "being" with "doing" and thereby avoided the time and space necessary to face ourselves. We do not know who we are.

Further, we are not who we were intended to be. The creation account in Genesis depicts humans as made in the image of God, that is, created for mutuality of relationship, joyful exuberance in worship, delight in our universe, in harmony with others, our world, and ourselves. That story stands in sharp contrast to the people we have become — alienated from others and fearful of what surrounds us.

A Great Chasm Is Fixed: Alienation from God

Most theologies begin with our alienation from God as the source of all other alienation. The Fall, Adam's original sin (which we have all inherited), is presumed to be the root cause. All other forms of alienation are dependent upon and grow out of this fundamental alienation.

If we accept this interpretation, the tendency is to rely upon purely religious or idealistic approaches to our predicament. This has been the predominant response of the church. It is because of this that we have such trust in pious individualism and so little trust or concern for what has been termed the social dimension of the gospel. If we understand the basic sin to be religious and metaphysical, then historical and material expressions of salvation seem less than important and all other forms of alienation can be considered as secondary and therefore treated lightly.

There is another interpretation that does more justice to the matter. The story of the Fall tells us of an alienation so total, so cosmic, so pervasive, that not one aspect of life is left untouched. In the light of it, we cannot think of our situation as a mere problem to be solved, but a catastrophe for the human condition. This is an accurate description of our situation. In the face of such total tragedy we are driven to a language that transcends manipulation, technique, and quick fixes.

In the Gospel of Luke (chap. 16) Jesus tells the story of a rich man and a sickly beggar named Lazarus. Lazarus was an outcast of society, lying daily at the door of the rich man's house, hoping for some of the crumbs that would be thrown out. The rich man, as was the custom of his day, had nothing to do with Lazarus. They both died. The rich man was sent to Hell, where he was tormented constantly. Looking upward to Heaven, he saw Lazarus resting peacefully in Abraham's bosom, an obvious contrast to his rejected and alienated station on earth. In his agony, the rich man pleaded with Abraham to send Lazarus with a drop of water to cool his tongue. Abraham responded, "Between us and you a great chasm has been fixed, in order that those who would pass from here to you may not be able and none may cross from there to us."

The great chasm between Heaven and Hell, between the God of beggars and the self-righteous, uncaring perpetrators of alienation, is fixed. All those who participate in causing alienation from others, our work, our world, ourselves are themselves alienated from the very ground of creation and the possibility of peace. We have no other words for the totality, depth, and ultimacy of this separation except to speak of it as alienation from God.

But this alienation does not begin with some historic metaphysical drama or some conscious decision to reject God. The alienation begins and ends with our relationships. Dorothee Soelle, drawing upon the mystical tradition within Judaism and Christianity, speaks of God as that which is "between us."[9] It is not necessary either to accept or reject the cosmology of early Christianity or Judaism in order to make sense of the claim that in hating our sister or brother we hate God (1 John 4). If we are alienated from others, our work, our world, ourselves, we are *ipso facto* alienated from God.

It is a matter of the starting point. Rooting our experiences of alienation in our separation from God, described as original sin or total depravity, is pure speculation. Rooting our doctrine of the great chasm between God and us in our concrete experiences of alienation is to face the depth of our situation with utmost seriousness.

Our alienations are interrelated. It is impossible to be alienated from our work without being alienated from others, to be alienated from others without being alienated from ourselves, to be alienated from our world without being alienated from God. It is simply good descriptive sense to talk about the tragedy of our situation as a chasm that is fixed between God and us.

Our condition is one of alienation. Its forms are varied and pervasive. We are cut off from others, our work, our world, our institutions, ourselves, and God. In every sense of the word, we are No People. We turn now to consider the means of our alienation, to explore the ways in which we have lost the fullness of our humanity and relationships.

Chapter 2

"Bricks without Straw": The Mechanisms of Our Alienation

When the Hebrews were slaves in Egypt the first request that Moses and Aaron made to Pharaoh was that they might be allowed to hold a feast in the wilderness to worship the God of Abraham, Isaac, and Jacob. Pharaoh not only rejected their request but heaped upon them the additional burden of having to make the bricks without the provision of straw. And so the people who were "No People" suffered increased oppression. In this incident are gathered the two essential means of alienation, the imposition of identity and the imposition of relationship.

Imposed Identities: The Implication of Inferiority

Memory has always been central to the people of Israel's self-understanding. Invariably, when the children of Israel sought to identify themselves, they went back to their origins. They spoke of themselves as the people of Yahweh who had been delivered "out of the land of Egypt, out of the house of bondage." At other times, they referred to themselves in terms of the patriarchs, or King David, or certain judges or prophets. They understood themselves to be part of a great tradition that gave special shape to their identity. They named themselves by the events of their own history. The "children of Abraham, Isaac, and Jacob" affirmed their nomadic roots. The "sons of Levi, Benjamin, and Judah" recognized their tribal roots. "The people of Zion" or the "House of David" indicated their nationhood and territorial claims.

But in Egypt their uniqueness was denied. The identity they bore was given to them by the slavemasters and it was an identity that made them nothing — no people. The very name "Hebrews" signifies the loss of specialness. It was a name given to numerous tribes who came from the geographic region across the Euphrates River. Their uniqueness was hidden by that name; there was nothing to indicate the specialness of their ancestry. It was the same when the slavemasters in the United States lumped all blacks under the name "Nigra" or "Negroe" or "Darkie," without reference to their specific African nationality and culture. The intention (often accomplished) was to wipe out the memory of a people.

This can be seen in the account of the burning bush, when Moses was called by God to be the deliverer of his people. In a fascinating interchange between God and Moses, Moses erects a series of barriers designed to allow him to escape from the calling. Or perhaps he was simply pointing to the realities of the situation. The first barrier Moses mentions has to do with the lost memory of his people. "If I come to the people of Israel and say to them, 'The God of your fathers has sent me to you,' and they ask me, 'what is his name?' what shall I say to them?" (Exod. 3:13) They had forgotten their fathers. There was no longer any power in the designation.

Upon his return from self-imposed exile, Moses begins the process of the liberation of his people. His first task is to remind them of their true identity. It is interesting to note that while Pharaoh continues to refer to the slaves as Hebrews, most of the time Moses refers to them as the children of Israel, designating their descent from Jacob and his father and grandfather, Isaac and Abraham.

The first request made to Pharaoh by Moses and Aaron was similarly linked with the question of identity. "Thus says the Lord, the God of Israel, 'Let my people go, that they may hold a feast to me in the wilderness'" (Exod. 5:1). Pharaoh's rejection of their request was an astute one. Though the request appears innocuous enough he correctly perceived the threat that such an action posed. (How often in our experience has worship presented a threat to the existing order?) It was imperative that the slaves did not call themselves by their true names. And so he rejected the request and doubled their burden by taking away the straw with which they made bricks, thereby forcing their attention upon sheer survival, a condition hardly conducive to discovering one's true self.

Pharaoh had learned the lesson that so many oppressors have subsequently come to know — the usefulness of imposing a false identity in order to suppress a person or a people. At the same time, this permits the oppressors and those who are the instruments of oppression to have easy consciences. We know the bitter story of the way in which the slaveowners systematically stripped the new slaves of their African identity and culture in an attempt to make them forget their former freedom. But its effect upon the slaveholder must have been significant as well. Certainly it is easier to enslave someone whose identity has been changed into that of a non-person. We saw this at work during the Vietnam War. Many a veteran has spoken of the way in which referring to the enemy as "gook" removed some of the humanity from those whom they were killing, making their deeds more tolerable.

Most imposed identities are far more subtle than the above examples. They involve a naming that is both formal and informal. The informal names are the more pervasive and commonplace, including such forms as epithets, stereotypes, slurs, nicknames, and diminutives. Whether formal or informal, the function of imposed identity is to define the other in terms of the namer. And to the extent that the person named accepts the imposed identity, i.e., names herself similarly, she has become the identity implied.

There are two basic alienating functions most common in the process of imposing identities: subservience and superfluousness. Subservience involves the subordination of a person for the sake of usefulness to another. The subservient person fundamentally exists for the sake of serving another. While there are positive images of self-chosen subservience, e.g., the Suffering Servant in Isaiah or Jesus' self-emptying (Phil. 2), alienating subservience is not chosen, it is imposed. To bear the imposed identity of subservience is to be reduced to a means, to existing for the sake of the namer.

Superfluousness is the excess beyond what is needed. It is

no longer useful, if it ever was. To bear the imposed identity of superfluousness is to be unwanted (the handicapped), capable of being ignored (the institutionalized), benignly neglected (the ending of special programs for the black community as per Senator Moynihan's recommendation), or even genocidally discarded (the Native Americans during our earliest period of national expansion). If subservience implies a reduction to functionality — existing simply as a means for another — then superfluousness implies a reduction to uselessness. Each of these forms of identity is determined by the user, the imposer of the identity, who decides and identifies whether another person or another thing is useful or useless.

One form of alienation is to be involved in a relationship in which one's identity is determined by its usefulness to the user. It is the reduction to a state of non-being, a state in which mutuality between entities that have their own integrity is denied; this reduction is perpetrated and perpetuated by the imposition of identities.

For many of us it has been difficult to understand this "fuss" over names, such as women refusing to take their husbands' names, or blacks changing their names, or Hispanics insisting that we learn to say their names properly. But when names are understood as powerful factors in subservience or superfluousness, perhaps we can understand better the criticalness of such concerns to persons seeking to claim their own identity and worth.

When we reflect upon the matter, we have seen numerous cases of subservience maintained by imposed names. In Western society women have traditionally been expected to take their husband's name. Even those who choose to keep their maiden name are only once removed from the problem of patriarchy, for by taking the name of their father the mother's lineage and identity are not reflected. The problem is that the assumption of the patriarchal name goes hand in hand with a society of male dominance. If we move beyond the formal name change there are countless epithets or slang names given to women that further reduce them to subservience, such as "chick" (the reduction to a domesticated animal), or some of the names that reduce them to bodily parts that fulfill male sexual needs. Women are also subject to being labeled with numerous diminutives such as "drum majorettes," implying that the standard is the male drum major. No wonder so many women are concerned about the implications of subservience that they experience through naming.

Blacks have suffered the same fate. Kunte Kinte's almost superhuman efforts to keep his African name was a dramatic portrayal of the use of a name either to subordinate or to free.[1] The more contemporary epithet of "boy" serves the same subservience function. The desperate/proud cry of "Black Power," which Stokely Carmichael made famous, was in recognition that the designations "Negroe," or "Nigger" were used by a white society to imply inferiority and hence the right to subordinate blacks.

One can observe the use of naming or designation to maintain subservience within various hierarchical structures as well. Note the occurrence common to many offices in which the boss is referred to as "Mr." but the staff are referred to by their first names. Or the use within the military of "Sir" to designate a superior officer, or the church's use of "Father" or "Reverend" for the clergy while the parishioners are referred to by their first names. While it is true that such usages are not always intended to maintain subservience, in fact they usually have that effect.

When Yahweh says to the people, "I have called you by my name," they have been raised to a new status, that of "a chosen people, a royal priesthood, a holy nation," called to serve all the nations of the earth, not through an imposed subservience but through a chosen servanthood. The contrast is extreme. The new identity is an invitation to service, not an imposition of subservience.

The other alienating function of naming is the implication of superfluousness, the state of being unnecessary. Millions within our society bear such a name.

One of the tragedies of our nation is the manner in which our elderly are treated. As opposed to many traditional societies in which respect is given the elderly in recognition of their wisdom and in gratitude for their contributions, ours are discarded. One of the reasons for this is that in a technological, information-oriented society knowledge is changing so rapidly that the quickness of youth is more valued than the integrating capacities that can come from experience and maturity. When a society places its trust in and values too highly the new, the possessors of wisdom become superfluous. And so we have designated the elderly as such.

One of the key designations of superfluousness is "retired." The implication is that one is withdrawn from circulation, retreating, giving up. One retires out-of-date library books. To be retired is to be discarded from the mainstream. That is why for so many, retirement means death, both psychically and physically. Being shut off from the opportunity to be productive after forty or fifty years in which work has been the primary source of identity comes as a shock to the system. The image conjured up by the name "retired" is one of an indolent person, wasting away, waiting for something to happen, essentially useless.

Welfare recipients have also been designated as superfluous. They are frequently viewed as the pariahs of our society who have no desire to work and who spend all their creative energies trying to figure out how to cheat at the welfare game, milking those of us who do work. They are generally loathed, so much so that the word "recipient" has often been replaced by the word "cheat." Even our president has engaged in the name-calling. They are a group whom most of the society wish would disappear.

There is a critical societal shift taking place in the rise of a permanent welfare class, and within that class people of color (predominantly black and Hispanic) are going from being subservient to being superfluous. Previously our society needed blacks as slaves and both blacks and Hispanics as unskilled laborers — last hired and first fired, kept in a ready pool called the unemployed. With the rise of technology and the inexorable decline of unskilled jobs, those formerly needed are becoming superfluous. Our welfare recipients, whether people of color or whites, are no longer necessary. No wonder that those who have witnessed and experienced genocidal policies toward their own people in the past fear the consequences of superfluousness today.

The question poor whites have to face is whether the rise of their own permanently unemployed or underemployed status represents a similar threat. Certainly color has not been decisive in making the elderly superfluous. Why should it be any different with respect to the permanently unemployed?

Many children of welfare recipients suffer their own process of becoming superfluous within our school systems. They are labeled the "dropouts," many of them so designated by teachers and administrators while they are yet quite young. This self-fulfilling prophecy has resulted in horrendous statistics. There are sections of New York City in which only 20 to 25 percent of the young people who begin high school finish. The majority are dropouts, treated as debris, fodder for delinquency and crime, the rejects of a Social Darwinian process that rewards the fittest and ignores the weakest.

There are others: "bag ladies," "street people," "retards," and "cripples." All these painfully remind us that there are millions in our society who bear names that imply their uselessness. If the truth were spoken, most would prefer that such people be done away with, or at least hidden away. That is why we have institutions: asylums, prisons, and homes for the elderly, the retarded, and the handicapped. All serve to remove the superfluous from our sight.

In the spring of 1983 I taught an ethics course to twelve prisoners at Sing Sing Correctional Facility in Ossining, New York. Each of them, enrolled in a master's program at our seminary, was a long-term prisoner, many serving life sentences. While working with these men, whom I initially feared but came to love, the relationship between one's identity and superfluousness was driven home to me.

Ted, one of the oldest men in the class, was taken to a nearby medical center for a heart catheterization. During our time of prayer at the beginning of class, a number of the men expressed their concern that Ted not be used for medical experimentation. Their experience had given them cause to believe this was a possibility.

That afternoon after class I went to the medical center to visit him. The facility, which is modern, attractive, and pleasant, is in sharp contrast to Sing Sing. At the main desk I was informed he was in a ward reserved for prisoners. I meandered through the center and took the elevator to the second floor wing to which I had been directed. As the door opened I was ushered into a waiting room that was barren except for one long bench. The walls were dingy and the paint was peeling. There was no trash can in the room and debris littered the floor. I walked to the guard's station, which was appropriately built for maximum security, and inquired about Ted. The guard informed me that he was in the operating room and would not be out of recovery for several hours, so I left a note for him.

As I was leaving the hospital I stopped in the gift shop to buy him some flowers. I picked out a bunch of red carnations and asked to have them delivered. I was informed that no flowers were permitted in the prisoner's ward. Incredulous, I asked the woman to check with the guard. Her check confirmed the prohibition.

The next day I phoned to inquire about Ted's condition. He had had a catheterization, nothing else, and was doing well, a nurse informed me. I asked to speak to the officer in charge, to explore the issue of the flowers. He informed me that the prohibition was to prevent guns or drugs from being smuggled in the dirt of a plant. "What about cut flowers in a clear glass vase?" I inquired. Appealing to his softer side, I continued, "Everyone loves flowers. I'm sure if you were sick you'd want to have them in your room, wouldn't you?" "Yes," he replied, "but he's different, he's a prisoner." Furious, I asked the guard if prisoners weren't people with feelings and needs just as ours. "No," he said, "they're prisoners!" Ted's designation made him superfluous to the guard.

The distinction between subservience and superfluousness is important. In the first instance, one is reduced to a means, but a means necessary for the functioning of a given person or society. In the second instance, one is reduced to uselessness, in which survival becomes paramount. That is why so many today fear genocide. The Native Americans in the United States were superfluous and so they were eliminated. In some cases, such as the Holocaust, the issue becomes more complex. In a certain sense Hitler used the Jews as his scapegoat, fanning the flames of racism as his means of gaining power. On the other hand, his doctrine of Aryan purity meant that Jewish blood must be eliminated in order for a pure race to emerge. The Jews may have served a short-term purpose as a rallying point for his madness, but in the long run they were unnecessary and undesirable. Can we not understand the fears for survival that grip so many of our brothers and sisters of color and so many Jews today?

The alienation we experience may be one of subservience or of superfluousness. In either case, one of the principal means of its perpetuation is the imposition of identities that imply inferiority.

Imposed Relations: The Structures of Alienation

But our alienation is not simply a matter of identity. If that were all that were involved then simply thinking about ourselves differently or renaming ourselves would suffice to end the alienation. But the lessons of history show us that there is more to the problem than this. For the Negro to choose the name "black" was an important step. But it has not eliminated the racism within our society. For women who keep their maiden names an often significant change in attitude and behavior results, but there can be no denying that such a change still leaves women in a second-class status. If Pharaoh had called the Hebrews by another name, but still forced them to build the bricks for Egypt, they would still have been slaves. Just as a rose by any other name is still a rose, so too is a slave.

We have had sufficient experience with the way in which shifts in designation have simply been a coverup for the same reality. "A totally revolutionary car" has been the description of something we can scarcely tell from the previous year's model. Outright lies are now labeled by our government as "misinformation." Weapons of war like the MX missile are called "Peacekeepers." The contras are called "Freedom Fighters." But these new designations do not change the facts.

While we spoke of the importance of imposed identities in the process of alienation and the need to find the name that authentically identifies one's true self, we dare not ignore the other side of the equation. Imposed relationships are also a fundamental means of perpetuating alienation. Relationships are the structures that govern our lives. They range from the highly personal, such as marriage or parent-child, to the more societal, such as citizen or worker. In each aspect of our lives we are set in a relationship that has the capability of contributing to our authentic humanity or of alienating us from the image of God.

The Hebrews were not only a people whose special history

and identity was denied through a process of naming. They were also slaves. Slavery is a property relationship among people. It is a relationship of domination and subordination that is maintained through compulsion. All forms of slavery demand some form of compulsion, whether military, economic, or ideological. Most demand all three. It was because of this compulsion that the final and decisive contest with Pharaoh was a military battle.[2] What began for the slaves as a demand for religious and cultural expression — "let us go out into the wilderness and hold a feast to the God of our heritage" — finally escalated into insurrection and flight during which the Egyptian army was defeated. The conflict escalated because the oppression was more than simply one of identity. It was an enforced slave relationship.

Many people, especially Christians, have been slow to recognize that social structures or relationships are means of perpetuating alienation. We have been quick to attack the slurs, stereotypes, and names that demean others, but we have been reluctant to address the realities of social, economic, and political structures. Such a limitation will not do, for hand in hand with our identities are the relationships in which we live.

Welfare recipients are not simply looked down upon and defined as superfluous. The welfare system as designed and functioning within our country creates and perpetuates a dependency relationship that comes close to guaranteeing the social uselessness of the recipient. (Unless, of course, we understand that the existence of welfare recipients creates a vast industry for a professional service class of bureaucrats.) The existence of many of our welfare recipients is related to an economy that is based upon a steady rate of unemployment. While the base has traditionally been set at around 4 percent of the work force as permanently unemployed, in recent years we have often seen that level over 7 percent.

This permanent pool of the unemployed is deemed necessary for production flexibility in a society that operates with a capitalist economic model. It provides a ready number of persons who can be drawn upon during peak demand periods. It also serves to dampen the ardor of workers who might be inclined to strike, knowing that there are so many without jobs waiting for the opportunity to take theirs. It is no secret, of course, that unemployment and underemployment (having a job that pays less than the poverty level) are experienced in significantly higher percentages by blacks and Hispanics than by whites. The largest group affected by welfare is women. Generally their role as the primary parent, coupled with the preference men have traditionally received in terms of hiring, advancement, and salary, has contributed to the swelling of the welfare roles with women. The dramatic increase of unemployed and underemployed women who have been forced onto welfare has led some to designate the problem as the "feminization of poverty."[3]

Since unemployment hits people of color most severely (last hired, first fired) and poverty finds its largest number of victims among women and children, it comes as no surprise that our welfare system is the dumping ground for millions of superfluous people. To designate welfare recipients as superfluous, however, is not enough. That might enable us to hide the racism and sexism of the situation. When we move beyond the imposed identity to the question of the structures or relationships of welfare, we are forced to face the stark fact that this means of alienation is gender and race specific. It is a relationship that perpetuates the superfluousness of women and people of color.

The superfluousness of many is maintained by a police, judicial, and penal system that sends a disproportionate number of blacks and Hispanics to prison. (Over 65 percent of all prisoners in the U.S. are people of color, while less than 20 percent of the total population is people of color). The prisons have become a dumping ground for the superfluous. The unimportance of the poor in our society is further maintained by housing laws and practices that foster displacement and homelessness, by an educational system that spends far more per child in the affluent suburbs than in our cities, contributing greatly to the dropout rate. Who needs convicts, homeless, unemployed, dropouts? They are superfluous and the structures help make them so.

Structures also serve as a means for maintaining subservience. We have already seen how women are reduced to subservient status by means of certain imposed identities. But it does not stop with identity. The relationships and structures that characterize our lives reinforce that reality. Until very recently, our economy has been built on the backs of women's unremunerated labor in the home (except during times of war when they were needed). They have been housewives, i.e., married to the house and reduced to chattel status. It is no mere coincidence that women are treated by many as property to be given and received — "who gives this woman to be married to this man?" Women had no vote in the United States until 1920, nor did they have economic rights upon divorce until the late 1800s.

While some of these aspects have been undergoing dramatic change, the subservience of women as sexual objects remains unabated. Any randomly selected hour of television commercials will confirm the use of women as bait in the selling of products. There is little doubt that the subservient place of women in our society is more than just a matter of identity. That is crucial. But so, too, are the relationships by which we organize our lives along the lines of gender.

The subservient position of blacks is likewise perpetuated by various relationships that go beyond questions of identity. The subservience implied by the designation "boy" may have been moderated somewhat as a response to the insistent demands of blacks that they be called by a name of their choosing. But their subservience is still a fact of life. Perhaps nowhere can this be seen more clearly than in South Africa's apartheid structure of relationships. Blacks are not superfluous there; quite the contrary. They are necessary to the economy. But they suffer at the hands of a white minority through such structures as Pass Laws, non-citizenship, enforced migration, and separation of families, all designed to maintain control over them as units of the production machinery.

Hispanics suffer structural as well as identity forms of alienation in this society. The structural forms are of both superfluousness and subservience. Those whom we don't want are termed "illegal aliens" and are hunted by border patrols and bounty hunters and, when discovered, sent home. We do not need any more foreigners who can't speak English swelling the ranks of our unemployed and receiving welfare so they are driven back across the border (as with the Mexicans). Their superfluousness is structured into our immigration laws.

The irony of this is that what has driven them to our shores for deliverance has been significantly caused by our nation's political and economic policies and practices. Many are fleeing repressive military dictatorships that we have helped bring to power and/or support (such as in Guatemala, El Salvador, Haiti, and the Dominican Republic). The majority have left economies of extreme poverty that have been seriously weakened by our government and U.S.-based multinational corporations. Our foreign policies and economic practices have consistently benefited us at the expense of Third World nations. Many of those countries have been turned into one-crop economies (such as coffee or bananas), which have eroded the normal agricultural base that had previously provided basic food supplies for the population. They are now required to import the foods that they used to raise, usually at significantly higher cost to them. In addition, the world banking system, primarily controlled by the United States through the International Monetary Fund and the World Bank, has fostered an indebtedness in these countries that demands that most of their money goes to paying off their foreign debts, leaving nothing for investment and development. The result of this exploitative relationship has been the disruption of the Third World economies, the predictable unrest of the poor, police repression in the name of law and order, and millions forced to flee their homes for economic or political survival.

As is the case with blacks and women, it is impossible to understand the plight of the superfluous or subservient Hispanics within our borders simply in terms of stereotypes or imposed identities. The relationships that govern their lives are central factors in the means of alienation.

Our retirees are subject to the same double whammy of imposed identities and relationships. The roles and productive activity that they have enjoyed most of their lives, and that have formed an important aspect of their meaning in life, have been taken away. Retirement means the removal of most opportunities for productive contribution to the society. Further, there is generally a significant drop in income, forcing people who were once proudly independent to become dependent upon others. Finally, the institutions that house and care for the elderly, which form an incredibly fast growing segment of our economy, gather together the society's cast-offs in a manner that reinforces their isolation and superfluousness. The increased mobility of our society, the larger number of working wives, and the increase in second and third marriages are all relationships or structural factors that contribute to the breakdown of the home-oriented care of the elderly that prevailed in times past.

Even those of us who do not fit into any of the above categories have experienced demeaning treatment at our work, whether as a cog in a large production machine, or a replaceable part within some large bureaucracy. We dare not be duped into thinking that our basic condition is changed by a simple change in title or name. That is a trick being played on increasing numbers of people today. Despite changes in designation to "professional" or "administrative assistant," the work continues to lack meaning or involve fundamental participation in decisions. Further, those of us who depend upon salaries (most of us) know that whatever rage or resolve to change things we may feel is usually thwarted by the stark reality that we are totally dependent upon that income and would be only weeks or months from bankruptcy without it. Our subservience in the workforce is a matter both of our identity and of the economic and bureaucratic relationships that govern our lives.

In effect, what we have in our society are three classes: the users, the used, and the useless. The first two are essential to the functioning of the economy. The users are those who control the relationships of the society and provide the identities by which people live. The used are those whose energies and skills serve the interests of the users. The third class, the useless, are cast aside. This class of useless or superfluous people is expanding steadily as the shift to technological and service-oriented industries continues.

To be subservient or to be superfluous are conditions of alienation. So, too, is the condition of being a user. Those who have the power to use others for their own benefit or to declare some to be useless have lost the basic relationship of mutuality and interdependence that is characteristic of the image of God. While there are substantial rewards associated with being a user, the cost is the same, namely, alienation. The means of the alienation that we each experience are imposed identities and relations of oppression.

In order for anything fundamentally different to occur, in order for alienation to be overcome, we must recognize and deal with both means of alienation, imposed identities and imposed relationships. We must understand and change both our identities and our relationships. Anything short of that will leave us as we are.

To understand and change only our identities will leave in place the basic structures that have, in the long run, the power to impose the identities. To understand and change only the relationships without naming ourselves in a new way will result in a simple shift of users, not in the elimination of the alienated relationship. Only to understand the identities and relationships that determine us without changing them reduces us to the world of mental gymnastics, pretending that things are different because we can talk about them. And finally, only to change the identities and relationships of alienation without the arduous discipline involved in understanding them fully will lead to the perpetuation of the same mistakes.

The task before us then is both to understand and to change both the identities and relationships of alienation. Before we can turn to that task, however, we must address the most common responses to alienation that prevent us from either understanding or changing ourselves and the situation.

Chapter 3

"Scattered over the Face of the Earth": False Responses to Alienation

While the biblical story begins in the Garden, the remainder of it concerns the response of God and humans to the reality of our alienation. Tragically, many of our responses have only exacerbated our condition because they are false. The Tower of Babel story is a graphic and archetypal account of these false responses.

> Now the whole earth had one language and few words. And as men migrated from the east, they found a plain in the land of Shinar and settled there. And they said to one another, "Come, let us make bricks, and burn them thoroughly." And they had brick for stone, and bitumen for mortar. Then they said, "Come, let us build ourselves a city, and a tower with its top in the heavens, and let us make a name for ourselves, lest we be scattered upon the face of the whole earth."... So the Lord scattered them abroad from there over the face of all the earth, and they left off building the city. Therefore its name was called Babel, because there the Lord confused the language of all the earth.... (Gen. 11)

To be scattered represented an enormous threat to the people of that time. It left them vulnerable to attack by roving bands of marauders who could easily overcome isolated individuals or families farming or herding cattle in the valleys and plains. In order to protect themselves from attack, they built fortified cities to which they could flee. Gradually, the cities became the centers for communication, culture, and commerce.

At the heart of many such cities was a temple tower that served both as a symbolic center of attention and also as a means of connecting with the gods. The Tower of Babel probably represents the proud achievements of the Babylonian and Assyrian kings who built temples "as high as the heavens."[1]

The attempt to solidify their position by trying to reach the gods is not hyperbole or myth, but coincides with the then current belief that the gods resided in various levels of the atmosphere. By building a structure high enough, it was thought to be possible to gain direct access to them and the concomitant blessings and unity that such connection guaranteed. The Genesis narrative underscores the inauthenticity of such an attempt to deal with the threat of disunity and scatteredness.

The tellers of the story realized that these kingly monuments represented the "ruthless power and oppression of the great empires"[2] and that such attempts at unifying civilization through dominance and grasping only made matters worse. In the story, God sees the ambitious undertaking to build a tower for what it is, namely, self-aggrandizement and dominance. In the face of such an attempt, God scatters the people over the face of the earth.

This is a constant theme of the Scriptures. The people who are lost, alienated from everything, seek to find their salvation only to end up in a condition worse than when they started. That is the central lesson of the story Jesus told about the man possessed by a demon:

> When the unclean spirit has gone out of a man, he passes through waterless places seeking rest, but he finds none. Then he says, "I will return to my house from which I came" and when he comes he finds it empty, swept and put in order. Then he goes and brings with him seven other spirits more evil than himself, and they enter and dwell there; and the last state of that man becomes worse than the first." (Matt. 12:43–45a)

Alienation is not necessarily removed because of our responses, even religious ones. In many cases today, the church has become a central, though unwitting, actor in the theater of alienation. Our theology has often served as a justification for the forms of alienation and our false responses to them, while our cultic, administrative, and pastoral practices have become structural means for reinforcing these forms and false responses. At the center of many of the false responses stands the tower of religion as it is practiced and as it is transmitted through doctrine.

Karl Marx correctly understood that the beginning of all criticism is the critique of religion. Rather than dismissing the importance of people's faith and practice, Marx affirmed its centrality. Because Marx thought that religion was an illusory way to deal with reality, he believed that if one eliminated the social conditions that gave rise to the illusion there would no longer be any need for religion. Marx was correct in his understanding that religion often serves as a coping mechanism that allows the basic conditions to remain the same. He was clearly wrong in his assumption that it would someday prove to be unnecessary for human existence, as is evidenced by its increasing vitality in China and Cuba as well as its tenacity in Russia. However, insofar as he was correct, we are compelled to examine our beliefs and practices in order to discover when and in what ways they contribute to the false response. Until we do this, we cannot move to the task of transformation.

We may build a city and a tower to solidify our position only to find ourselves scattered upon the face of the earth. In order to avoid this fate, we do well to consider some of the false responses to our alienation as they appear within both society and the church today.

Resignation to Fate

When faced with circumstances that seem intractable, despite our most heroic efforts, it is quite natural to feel overwhelmed and out of control. It is as if a power beyond our ability to influence has the reins and all our attempts are futile. Fatalism involves a sense of inevitability and impotence to change things. We encounter a sense of fatalism in almost every realm of our lives today.

In every battle I have been involved in regarding issues of housing, jobs, military cutbacks, racism, or educational reform, the odds have been stacked against us. And in every battle there were some individuals who gave up in resignation, stating, "You can't fight city hall."

Flying from Brazil to the States I sat next to a Brazilian engineer who was lamenting the destruction in the Amazon River basin as a result of the industrial development there. Though he felt it was a disaster, his conclusion was that "you can't stop progress."

These examples could be multiplied. "What do you expect of a woman?" — as if all women were alike and all behaviors were determined by gender. "Life is like that" — as if history and human nature were fixed in concrete. "What can you expect at her age?" — as if a certain number of years automatically guarantees a certain level of maturity or capacity. With fatalism there is a pervasive sense that things are fixed, determined by some inner principle or some external force that inevitably leads to a predictable end.

This kind of fatalism is not new. It has been with us from time immemorial. It has been the foundation for many religions, especially those that are predominantly nature religions.[3] The essential responsibility of humans in the face of dominant and apparently unchangeable realities, such as the seasons, the tides, or the weather, is to conform to the patterns that have been set. Human history then parallels natural history. Roles set by the accident of birth (royal succession or the place of women) are assumed to be divinely ordained. If there is a time and a place for everything in nature, there is a time and a place for everything and everyone within history. Ecclesiastes echoes this understanding.

Fatalism today takes two forms: pessimistic and optimistic. We are most familiar with the former, captured in the aphorism "life is a rat race," which implies a predetermined course set by others, going nowhere despite much activity. In the religious realm many dismiss the possibility of any fundamental change in the condition of the starving millions by proclaiming that "it's God's will," or invoking the words of Jesus, "The poor you will always have with you" (Matt. 26:11). The latter quote, when so used, is taken out of both its context in Jesus' time and its context in the Hebrew Scriptures from which Jesus was quoting. Jesus was saying that there would be continuous opportunity for assisting the poor and it was quite appropriate to bestow a loving gift upon one who was about to die. The Scripture from which he was quoting (Deut. 15) promises that poverty shall not exist if the people obey the word of God (Deut. 15:4, 5). The only reason for continued poverty is their unfaithfulness. Pessimistic fatalism is a resignation to a condition we would not have selected had we the choice.[4]

Optimistic fatalism is equally resigned, but in this case to a direction assumed to be benevolent, although inevitable. It is epitomized by the slogan "you can't stop progress." There are two basic assumptions behind such a response. The first is that there is a fixed direction that is beyond our ability to control, even if we wanted to. The second is that the direction of things is essentially progressive and any negative developments are simply ancillary costs to be borne for a greater good. Living with the threat of nuclear accident is seen as the acceptable by-product of the utilization of nuclear (fission) energy.

The tragedy of fatalistic responses is that we are prevented from either imagining or working toward overcoming our alienated state. We have seen this tragedy over and over again: in "tracking" children from their earliest school years toward college, manual labor, or drop-out; in the political/economic policy of triage, which assumes that the starving, weaker members of the human race must be allowed to die for the sake of the survival of the fittest; or in the resigned couple who merely co-exist for years because they are convinced that there is no other possibility.

Unfortunately, some aspects of Christianity have contributed to this fatalistic response. As one raised in the Calvinist tradition, both in its fundamentalist Baptist form and later as a Presbyterian, the doctrine of election played a dominant role in my development. My earlier fundamentalist tradition included an extreme form of this doctrine, that is, double predestination: the preselecting by God of some to heaven and some to hell. In retrospect, one can see how this allowed us the freedom to accept gratefully the benefits of being white, religious, and Protestant in the 1950s while remaining unconcerned about the unemployed or hungry. Each person was thought to be fulfilling God's intended role. Our position lacked the subtlety of Calvin's notion that God has ordained some to be poor so that others might be allowed the ministry of generosity.

Calvin's teachings, of course, are far more ambiguous than to lend easy credence to such an interpretation even though some of his followers adhered to such ideas. One must understand Calvin's thought as a corrective to the dominant Roman Catholicism of his day, which emphasized works in such a way as to manipulate its adherents into a dubious casuistry (a system for dealing with all cases of morality with specific directives) and a dependency upon the church as the controller of the means of grace. Calvin's emphasis upon the sovereignty of God stood in marked contrast to the assumptions either that one could merit salvation through works or that the church could control salvation.

While Calvinism has at times served as an impetus for change (for example, in the rise of capitalism or the Puritan revolution in England),[5] it has probably been best known popularly for its emphasis upon total depravity. Calvin's development of the notion of total depravity picks up on the Augustinian and Pauline emphasis upon our sinful condition, which is so severe as to prevent us from doing anything that could merit salvation. In contrast to the Jewish emphasis upon *mitsvoth* (good deeds) or Roman Catholicism's understanding of the continuity between nature and grace making good works a possibility for all, stands Augustine and his assessment of the human condition captured in the famous dictum, *Non posse non pecare* (it is not possible not to sin). For Calvin and this tradition, the emphasis upon God's sovereign freedom is dependent upon the equally strong emphasis upon our unworthiness, our inability to merit salvation. In most churches, including my own Presbyterian denomination, the positive emphasis on God's sovereignty, especially in terms of election, has taken a back seat, but we've kept alive the negative pole of the equation, namely, our total depravity. This is an ironic and unfortunate development.

In this context it is not surprising that Karl Barth's emphasis upon the total otherness of God and the impossibility of human knowledge or effort to bridge that gap has often provided a basis for fostering fatalism. While it is clear that Barth intended no such consequence (he was an active proponent of socialism and an avid enemy of fascism), it has been an easy move from his orthodox emphasis upon our depravity to the kind of quietism and resignation so characteristic of mainstream churches today.

Not all Christians subscribe formally to the doctrine of total depravity, but the secularized version of it is rampant both within and outside the church. People are assumed to be essentially untrustworthy and prone to evil. One of the most frequent responses to attempts to bring about radical change (e.g., the elimination of poverty through new economic or political forms, or the overthrow of a malevolent dictator, or the elimination of nuclear arms) has been despair that there is no point in making basic changes since the new people in power will end up repeating the same injustices. With such a mind-set any thought of change is doomed.

Such pessimism, while warranted on the balance scale of history, leaves no room for the exception, for the miracle of conversion, for resurrection surprise. All change is seen as a simple transfer of oppressors, not as a transformation of persons and conditions.

The teachings of our churches often reinforce this fatalism. Our hymns (the source of much of our common theology) are filled with aspersions about our depravity: "such a worm as I," "sinking deep in sin." Our sermons and educational material teach of the original sin of Adam, which all have inherited and which makes us totally unworthy. Our ritual of confession is an amorphous generalization about our guilt that by its lack of specificity reinforces a sense of the total pervasiveness of our sin. "We acknowledge and bewail our manifold sins and wickedness which we, from time to time, most grievously have committed, by thought, word, and deed, against thy Divine Majesty."[6]

Confession is critical, but confession of this sort is counterproductive. At best it is excuse-making of the most innocuous sort. Such a confession sounds like a cover-up. At worst, if the confessor genuinely feels the remorse implied in this repetitive and amorphous ritual, she would have to come away feeling as if there were no good within her.

There is a way to understand sin as radical without falling into fatalism, as I shall discuss in chapter 5. In the meantime, the point here is simply that the emphasis upon total depravity, in a context that fosters despair about fundamental transformation, has led many to a sense of hopelessness about any efforts to change our situation.

A second major contributor to a sense of fatalism within the church has been the way in which we treat the Bible. The Scriptures are a written compilation of the collective witness of God's people to God's gracious acts in our midst. Too frequently they have become a textbook for prescribing correct acts and thoughts, a handbook of orthodoxy.

In his classic study of the philosophy of science Thomas Kuhn explains how scientific explanations or theories (he calls them paradigms) are compiled in textbooks and used in a manner that implies that they contain the final word about things.[7] The problem, he points out, is that despite the rapid expansion of data that make old theories inadequate, students are taught textbook paradigms as if they were still operable. Perhaps even more important, rather than discovering and creating their own paradigms in a true scientific fashion, students are reduced to receiving the explanations of others as truths fixed for all time.

The Scriptures are treated in a similar manner by many Christians even though the Scriptures themselves preclude such a closed approach. They are a constantly developing response to God's relationship with a living community. Within the Bible we have an unfolding and changing understanding of God, the universe, and ourselves. The continuity that is inherent does not preclude change and development.

Historically, both the Hebrew Scriptures and the New Testament were a constantly developing corpus. With the closing of the canon in the fourth and fifth centuries the ongoing nature of the written witness was lost. In response to various heresies, the church fathers fixed an authoritative body of texts as the rule ("canon" means "rule" in Latin) by which all disputes would be judged.

Approaching the Scriptures as a closed book possessing the final statement on all matters of faith and practice is similar to treating the Bible as a textbook rather than as an authoritative and faithful witness to what has transpired to date, or as a building block to the discovery of new truth. When so understood, the believer (student) accepts the Bible (textbook) as a truth fixed in time, and thus must forcibly apply previously workable explanations to new situations. Such an approach leads to a closed view of history and truth and fosters a fatalism about change.

Of course almost no one can live with such rigidity, and hence we make compromises. Even after the closing of the canon, believers throughout the ages have "tampered" with it. Luther considered the book of James to be an "epistle of straw" not worthy of inclusion in the Bible. Calvin also ignored certain books in his Commentaries. But despite these and others questions about the canon, the notion of a fixed text that contains all that is necessary for faith and practice has been the prevalent approach to Scripture.

As Luther and Calvin, we have "a canon within the canon." We decide that certain portions of Scripture need to be reinterpreted or even ignored (e.g., the death penalty prescribed for homosexuality in Leviticus 20:13, or the prohibition against women speaking in church in 1 Corinthians 14:34). Despite the fact that most of us are constantly involved in reinterpretation of Scripture, there remains a myth of its fixity, the idea that it conveys unchanging truth for all situations and all times. When we succumb to such an idea we are limited to conformity to the prescriptions from the past. While some of those prescriptions may still be applicable and many of its descriptions about life still valid, our responsibility is for the ongoing discovery of God's intent for our time, and this responsibility cannot be fulfilled by simple acceptance of Scripture as textbook. Our task is an ongoing one that must be constantly worked out communally by each generation, in dialogue with the witness of those who have gone before. Text and context interact to reveal the truth. It is the absence of this open dialogue that I have observed so often in the churches' dealing with the Bible.

When the Bible is taught and transmitted to us through sermons, church school, hymns, liturgy, and customs as a fixed body of truth, we are reduced to fatalistic respondents, removed from the responsibility of discovering ongoing revelation. We thereby reinforce the prevailing societal response of fatalism in the face of alienation.

Resignation to our condition because we believe it is inevitable may offer an ease that comes with avoiding struggle, but it is a false ease that only guarantees the perpetuation of our alienation.

Denying the Problem

Unable to confront the reality of his condition, Willie Loman denied his discouragement, rejections, and failures. He lived in a world of illusions and delusion. When confronted with the fact that he had not sold anything for some time and had been borrowing money from a friend in order to appear to have an income, he fabricated excuses that allowed him to believe that a dramatic "big deal" was just around the corner. In order to avoid the painful truth about his thirty-four-year-old son, Biff, who was a thief and a drifter, he made up success stories about him. Many, like Willie, seek to escape the pain of alienation by denying it.

Sociologists and psychologists tell us that denial is one of the principal ways in which people handle dissonance in their lives. Cognitive dissonance is the discrepancy between the way we expect or think things will occur — or believe they should be or want them to be — and the way they actually are.[8] People cannot willingly live with such dissonance and generally seek ways to reduce it, usually by changing their perceptions, beliefs, expectations, and values. In far fewer cases they seek to change the circumstances that created the dissonance. Rather than shattering his self-image and hopes, Willie Loman distorted the facts and made excuses.

There is incredible resistance to seeing matters as they really are. The Hebrew prophets were dealt with harshly because they attempted to break through the veil of denial that the nation and its leaders had erected to protect themselves from the pain of facing the truth. Many of the prophets were imprisoned, exiled, and ridiculed for their efforts to unveil the truth.

Denial of our condition is rampant today. Drug and alcohol abuse abound. The leisure industry permits the affluent to buy escape from the drudgery of their lives, vicariously living out the life of a "jock" or of a rich person. Television and movies provide escapist material that carries us to an illusory world of success and luxury (*Dynasty, Falconcrest,*) or effective retribution against evil (*Rambo, The Equalizer,*).

The denial runs deeper, however, than simply our private forms of escape. There are social mechanisms that seek to deny the truth of our alienation by hiding it.

FALSE RESPONSES TO ALIENATION

In a television documentary in the mid 1970s that focused on youth gangs and the police in the South Bronx, Anthony Buza, the district commander of the South Bronx police, lamented the sorry state of affairs in his district and the tragic transformation of his young cops into hardened enemies of the people whom they had initially come to serve. He described their role as running an army of occupation similar to that which the United States had in Vietnam. To the extent that he did the job he'd been hired to do, he considered that he was failing his country, for he had been hired to keep silent that which should be heard and to keep invisible that which should be seen.

When the silenced and hidden consequences of our alienation come into the open, as occurred during the rebellions in our cities in the 1960s or as is currently happening in South Africa, the veil of denial is torn asunder and, as in the days of the prophets, we want to expel those who shatter our myopia. Our society would seem to prefer to maintain the silence and invisibility.

The church has been a major factor in promoting denial. Some doctrines have been interpreted in an idealistic manner so that only the intangible is considered important or real while anything physical or material is considered secondary. Teaching about the future or end times (eschatology) has often fallen into this trap, emphasizing escape from the present through a hope in "pie in the sky bye and bye." By emphasizing the transitory and even illusory nature of our current experience and fixing our sights on the return of Jesus and a Kingdom in another place, the reality or the importance of our present suffering is denied.

Another doctrinal interpretation that has fostered denial is found in the neo-orthodox understanding of what has been accomplished in the Resurrection. Karl Barth says,

> In the Resurrection of Jesus Christ the claim is made that God's victory, in the person of his Son, has already been won. Easter is indeed the great pledge of our hope, but simultaneously this future is already present in the Easter message. It is the proclamation of a victory already won. The war is at an end.... The game is won, even though the player can still play a few further moves.... It is in this

interim space that we are living, the old is past, behold it has all become new.[9]

For Barth, everything significant for history has been accomplished with the historic act of the Resurrection. The future is completed; the Resurrection and parousia are two events for us, but one event for God.[10] All that remains for us is the recognition of this fact.[11] In so claiming, Barth would not deny the reality of present evil and suffering, but rather deny its final power over our lives. For him, there was an incredible freedom to challenge all existing structures because of this accomplished fact. However, for many who have inherited Barth second hand, this teaching has become an excuse for denial of the power of evil and alienation as it is experienced now, for when all is said and done, what goes on now doesn't have ultimate significance.

Perhaps the most pernicious form of denial operative within the church today is "feel-good" religion. The liturgy, which is the dramatic re-enactment of the life, death, and resurrection of Jesus, has been replaced with a religion of hype, of good feelings. We have crystal palaces that inspire us, music that lifts us, sermons that titillate us, and prayers that assure us of the fulfillment of our desires. We have changed worship from serious drama into trivial entertainment.

Such criticism does not reject the place of joy, reassurance, and hope in worship. Black worship, for example, has incorporated those characteristics, but it has done so along with tears for the tragedy of our condition, sober appraisal, and prayerful groaning that gives authenticity to the positive dimensions of the worship. The essential difference here is between worship as denial and worship as refuge from an undeniable threat.

Much of mainstream religion and fundamentalism offers optimism instead of hope. The gospel offers hope, not optimism. Optimism denies the depth of the struggle, anticipating an inevitable happy conclusion. Optimism is based on a wish and ignores the realities of the present. Hope is based in history and takes the present condition with utmost seriousness. Optimism tells us things are getting better. Hope lives a life of conflict against the forces of death in the assurance that out of the conflict life can prevail. Based on a sober assessment of history, our alienation seems as pervasive and tragic today as it has in times past. There is no cause for optimism, except through denial.

The gospel of optimism is at the core of our "feel-good" religion. We are offered ecstasy, inner joy and peace, and assurance and knowledge of inevitable victory by religious cheerleaders who whip up a Superbowl-like frenzy. Such good feelings are seldom sustained. They are like the mountaintop ecstasy that soon dims as we return to the drudgery of the valley. With the return to the commonplace we feel betrayed as the good feelings fade with the revival of the testing. The tragedy of denial is that we only drive the forces of alienation deeper into the fabric of our society, making transformation all the more difficult and all the more wrenching.

Blaming the Victim

In the time of Jesus there was a fairly large class of people characterized by their poverty, disease, physical handicaps, and social undesirability. Known as "outcasts," "publicans," "sinners," or "unclean," they were forced into begging in order to survive. The majority of citizens responded to their presence by labeling, ostracizing, and blaming them for their condition. It was assumed that their state was due to their sinfulness, or to the sin of their forebears. This is the background of the story in which the Pharisees asked Jesus concerning a physically handicapped man, "Who sinned, this man or his father?" (John 9). Scandalizing the people of his time, Jesus claimed these outcasts as his own people, incurring the same ostracism and rejection. In calling them his people and the children of God, he became one of the victims, rather than their accuser.

William Ryan had suggested a contemporary counterpart to the treatment of the biblical outcasts, which he calls "Blaming the Victim."

> The generic process of Blaming the Victim is applied to almost every American problem. The miserable health care of the poor is explained away on the grounds that the victim has poor motivation and lacks health information. The problems of slum housing are traced to the characteristics of tenants who are labeled as "Southern rural migrants"

not yet "acculturated" to life in the big city. The "multi-problem" poor, it is claimed, suffer the psychological effects of impoverishment, the "culture of poverty," and the deviant value system of the lower classes; consequently, though unwittingly, they cause their own troubles. From such a viewpoint, the obvious fact that poverty is primarily an absence of money is easily overlooked or set aside.[12]

While maintaining our posture of humanitarianism and love for the "deserving poor," we nonetheless manage to respond to the alienation of millions of victims by blaming them. One has only to look at our welfare system to see the alienation maintained through victim blaming in the context of a program supposedly designed to help the victims. In the face of massive poverty, increased unemployment, and dislocation due to "development," we continue to blame people for needing welfare. In the face of rules that make it impossible to receive Aid for Dependent Children if there is a father living in the house, we continue to blame women for having babies without husbands. In the face of a bureaucratic structure that makes it almost impossible to maintain one's composure, let alone one's dignity, we continue to blame people for trying to beat the system.

Such a response removes the burden of any fundamental changes, either within our society or among our relationships. Ryan says that the process of victim-blaming is ideological (i.e., it serves as a rationalization for the current relationships) and enables those who are not suffering from a particular alienation to remain safely entrenched in the status quo.

According to Ryan, the characteristics of an ideology are as follows:

> First, there is the belief system itself, the way of looking at the world, the set of ideas and concepts. Second, there is the systematic distortion of reality reflected in those ideas. Third is the condition that the distortion must not be a conscious, intentional process. Finally, though they are not intentional, the ideas must serve a specific function: maintaining the status quo in the interest of a specific group.[13]

This ideology of blaming the victims and the social programs

FALSE RESPONSES TO ALIENATION

that go hand in hand with such an ideology involve the assumption that "individuals 'have' social problems as a result of some kind of unusual circumstances — accident, illness, personal defect or handicap, character flaw or maladjustment — that exclude them from using the ordinary mechanisms for maintaining and advancing themselves."[14]

In this exceptionalist approach the individual is seen as the problem and attention is diverted from the relevant social structures. Blaming the victim is one of the most prevalent forms of dealing with alienation in our society.

The irony of this response is that it turns upon us. It is not only others who are to blame but also ourselves. In a classic study of working-class whites in the Boston area, Sennett and Cobb found self-denigration and unwarranted guilt to be common.[15] So many of us assume fault for the unachieved accomplishments, shattered dreams, unemployment, and other failures of our lives.

This is not only true of working-class people. Parents feel guilt over the direction of their children. Some guilt may be appropriate, but the media, schools, peer groups, and other factors contribute to shaping our children. Similarly, many women, rather than recognizing the circumstances that have narrowly circumscribed their world, have come to think of themselves as inferior to men. For many, blaming oneself is simply another form of blaming the victim.

The church is responsible, too, for victim-blaming and producing guilt. As mentioned earlier, the doctrine of sin as original and total plays a large part in maintaining guilt. If all of us are so fallen, certainly we must deserve whatever we get. Blessings are from God, but alienation comes from us.

Further, a focus upon rules as a predominant way of being religious contributes to guilt. At times, both Judaism and Christianity have placed rules at the center of their tradition, whether in the form of the Ten Commandments, the Talmud, Roman Catholic casuistry, or fundamentalist moralism. This rule orientation fits well with the prevailing social ethos of blaming the victim. Of course rules and discipline are appropriate, as we shall explore later, but what passes for Christian discipline in many churches is actually a form of moralism whose principle consequence is not faithful behavior, but inordinate guilt.

Third, the practice of confession, as experienced by many of us, also contributes to the mentality of victim-blaming. In a society in which we blame others and ourselves for matters beyond our control, to constantly repeat the fact that we are "miserable offenders," or "there is no good within us," cannot help but reinforce the expectation or sense that whatever has gone wrong involves our culpability. The victims are reinforced in their self-depreciation by such a rite.

In addition to lumping all people together in an undifferentiated responsibility, the ritual of confession in most churches avoids specificity about the sins that we confess, resulting in an amorphous sense of guilt. By failing to involve a specific focus to our confession or a careful analysis of the causal factors, we can avoid placing appropriate responsibility; it becomes a simple step to blame the victim.

The advantage of the private confessional is that it permits the individual to become specific about what is being confessed and even to explore how to change the situation. The disadvantage is that it can reinforce the hierarchical order of salvation by giving a priest the power to pronounce forgiveness. It was this form of abuse that was so prevalent a factor in the rise of the Reformation.

Corporate confession, rooted in the priesthood of all believers, is important for several reasons. First, when confession is simply a private matter, the victim can remain locked into a sense that the situation or condition is uniquely his or hers. Corporate confession removes the isolation of our plight and can begin to move us toward solidarity with each other. Second, to understand the nature of what we are confessing, we need the help of the broader community. Limited to our own perspectives, we easily fall into victim-blaming.

Appropriate confession should incorporate the best of both the private and corporate approaches, in a single process that involves careful study and analysis, specificity of focus, and the opportunity for people to engage in intimate sharing and even confrontation. It needs to be seen as part of the entire life of the faith community, involving group study, prayer, and sharing, as well as formal liturgical expressions.

Anything less than this will contribute to the extension of victim-blaming. When we blame others for what they did not create, the result is a further level of alienation between us and them. When we blame ourselves for what is inappropriate, we waste our energy trying to prove ourselves as worthy. All forms of victim-blaming do nothing to alleviate the condition of alienation. Quite the opposite, they drive us further from the possibility of reconciliation.

Keeping Busy

When the final days of Jesus' life were ominously drawing to a close, he was gathered with a few of his followers in a secluded spot. Judas' kiss of betrayal signaled the waiting soldiers to seize Jesus in order to carry him off to prison and trial. In a fury, one of Jesus' disciples leapt out and cut off the ear of the high priest's slave. Jesus rebuked him and healed the man's ear (Luke 22:47-51).

There come times of such frustration that we feel we must do something, anything. We can imagine how the disciple felt, but in this case, the action was both inappropriate and ineffective. Jesus' response has traditionally been taken as a repudiation of violence, and perhaps it was. Other events in his life, however, lead us to question such an interpretation, e.g., the forcible driving out of the moneychangers from the Temple. Whatever else the reasons for Jesus' repudiation of the violent act, it was also prompted by the ineffectiveness of trying to defend him in the face of such power. Further, the object of the action was inappropriate, a slave who was doing his master's bidding. The action did not address the basic actor, who was the master.

We are a pragmatic, activistic society. Doing something is usually considered better than doing nothing. Doing more is thought to be better than doing less. At the personal level we find ourselves turning to activities in order to prevent ourselves from facing the depth of our reality. We turn on the television, have a drink, pop a pill, work, play, anything to keep busy. How many failing marriages have been held together inauthentically by activism: having a baby, buying a new home or furnishings, a whirling round of entertainment, or even sex?

There is a distinction between strategic, effective action that is based on a sober assessment of the situation, and mere activism. The building of the tower of Babel simply could not address the problem, yet it involved tens of thousands in activity for years. There are times when it is appropriate only to pray, reflect, or analyze. There are times when it is appropriate simply to be. But in a fast-moving society such as ours, the tendency is to create a new program, do a new deed.

Many of the promises to correct the ills of our society are founded upon this mindless activism. We have had twenty plus years of so-called urban renewal that offered hopes of renewed cities, housing and jobs for the poor, only to discover that urban renewal, whether intended by its promulgators or not, came to mean "Negro removal."

Thomas Edison is reputed to have had an aphorism hanging above his desk, "Everything comes to he who hustles while he waits." Without an appropriate waiting, our action will prove self-defeating. We need the waiting that is characteristically referred to as spirituality and the waiting that is characteristic of good theory and analysis; both are essential. Activism is action without waiting. It only leads us deeper into our alienation.

Yet many forms of Christianity foster a mindless activism through both doctrine and practice. Even within Protestantism, which has assiduously rejected works as playing any role in our salvation, there has steadily crept back an ethos of activism that is barely distinguishable from the works righteousness so fiercely denounced by Luther, Calvin, and the other reformers. There is a certain way of thinking about holiness that contributes to inauthentic activism. Understanding God as the Holy One has been expressed in two basic forms within Christianity, the subjective and the ethical. Obviously it is impossible finally to separate these two strains, but emphasis has usually been upon one or the other, sometimes to the disparagement of the other.

The subjective form places its emphasis upon our experience of the Holy as a feeling. This is exquisitely captured in Rudolph Otto's phrase, the *mysterium tremendum*,[16] a sense of overwhelming awe, and in the beatific vision of the mystical tradition in which one is totally caught up in the contemplation and experience of God's presence.

The ethical form has emphasized the concept of purity, e.g., the Holiness Code of Leviticus, the Psalmist's calls to moral purity (Psalm 1), or the moralistic codes of many contemporary churches. When "being holy" means being pure, with a private moralistic emphasis, we are continuously compelled to fulfill certain obligations. Such a moralistic emphasis has a tendency to underscore our necessity to be constantly on the go.

The concern to purify oneself easily leads to a concern to purify the world, which can become the kind of moralistic tyranny so prevalent today. Campaigns are mounted to prohibit the use of alcohol, censor books, enforce prayer in the schools, ban the right to choose abortion. The problem with this moralistic activism is that it fails to recognize the roots of alienation and simply endeavors to compel individuals (through legislation, persuasion, or intimidation) to act differently, without addressing the fundamental causes of their behavior.

Liberal Christianity has generally avoided such a concern for personal purity. As a religion of the more affluent, liberal Christianity has emphasized other kinds of acts, for example *noblesse oblige* or charitable deeds of the privileged ranks. For this kind of Christianity, stewardship has been replaced by philanthropy.

In stewardship one recognizes the source of all that one enjoys as resting with another. Whatever we enjoy is not ours to possess, but rather it is ours as a responsibility to manage carefully.

Philanthropy, by contrast, despite its etymology (meaning love of humans), has come to mean the giving away of our excess, at our discretion. While some sense of obligation may attend philanthropy for some, it is more often accompanied by a desire to be good or to do good, usually in the eyes of others, if not in the eyes of God.

The philanthropic mentality leads us to believe that our acts or good deeds or generosity are the result of our own doing, without remainder, and that we are the better for such deeds. Hence we tend to act in situations of alienation out of our largesse and feelings of sympathy, giving for the starving of Africa or providing shelters for the homeless of our cities. But there are several problems with such an approach.

The first problem is that when our feelings dictate our actions, as the feelings change so too can our commitments. Hence we can follow the fads that seem to change with whims. One has only to trace the history of social action and philanthropy among the wealthy, the foundations, and our denominations over the last twenty-five years to see evidence of such fadish behavior. Three- to five-year cycles have occurred around Civil Rights, the movement against the war in Vietnam, women's issues, gay rights, disarmament, each shift replacing the former focus, and each shift generating initial enthusiasm and publicity, frantic activity, and eventual burn-out or loss of interest. The same can be said of many congregations and individual Christians.

The second problem with religious philanthropy as inauthentic activism is that it has proven to be ineffective. Despite billions of dollars and enormous energy directed to addressing the alienation of our world, conditions seem little changed, if at all. So long as philanthropy prevails over stewardship as the basic form of Christian response, no fundamental transformation in the plight of the hungry, the homeless, or the poor will be effected.

Keeping busy is not a solution to our alienation. It may provide us a momentary sense of accomplishment, but when the dust has settled, we shall discover that things remain as before.

Hope in Magic

The prophet Jeremiah lived during a time of great upheaval in Judah. The threat of captivity by Babylon was imminent when Zedekiah came to the throne. As was customary in those times, there were magicians who sought to foresee and/or control the future through sorcery and witchcraft. Most of them sought to assure the nation and the king that their future could be secured by standing strong against any Babylonian incursion. The "spirits" had so indicated this to them and they would guarantee the outcome of the war.

But Jeremiah rejected such hope in magic, relying instead upon prayer and solid political analysis. His understanding of the situation led him to challenge these false prophets and to warn the king and the people not to take up arms but to take on the yoke of Babylonian captivity. Jeremiah's word was not comforting to a nation about to be invaded, and so it was rejected.

The ensuing battles proved Jeremiah to have been correct in his assessment. Because of their resistance, Jerusalem was destroyed and the nation's leaders, along with Jeremiah, were

FALSE RESPONSES TO ALIENATION

exiled. The entire fabric of the society was torn asunder because the people listened to the false prophets. Their alienation was increased horrendously because they trusted in magic.

Magic is the process by which we control outcomes through the use of certain formulas, elements, or rituals. If the right motions are gone through in the right manner, the rabbit will indeed emerge from the hat every time. We are a nation that hopes in magic. Persons who live in poverty and many of us who live from month to month by our wages play the numbers or buy lottery tickets, dreaming of the day when our lives will be transformed. We buy books that provide formulas for successful living, revitalization of our sexual relations, or instant fortunes through investment. The rash of speculative investment today exhibits this same hope. We are all hoping for Willie Loman's "big killing," which never comes for most of us.

Magic replaces careful thought and hard work with unexamined rote behaviors assumed to guarantee the desired outcome. Much of our current military preparation is packaged for the public in terms of magical notions about guarantees of deterrence or mastery. However, close examination reveals an illusory security with the most horrifying possibilities coming closer and closer to actualization. Since we hope so stubbornly in magic we continue to believe that more bombs will secure peace. The logic of our escalation bears more relation to sleight of hand than to reality.

The church is one of the master perpetuators of magic in a society that offers its alienated constant illusory hopes. This magic is worked through both doctrine and practice.

Our approach to the sacraments is often magical, as Juan Luis Segundo points out. In talking about Roman Catholicism, he says that "the infallible conferral of grace leaves room for some people, who seek to find a special privilege in the Church, to imagine that in the sacraments they have an instrument of grace which they can manipulate."[17] Its infallible quality is linked with the mechanical and the automatic. And so by degrees this nonphysical mechanism is degraded to the automatism and impersonal nature of the magical.

His critique is equally applicable for much of Protestantism. While many Protestants may consider the doctrine of transubstantiation as magic (the belief that in the Eucharist the elements of bread and wine are changed into the actual body and blood of Jesus, and hence are a means of grace), we tend to have our own form of magic — the Lord's Supper as the automatic unifier. Within my own experience, the emphasis of the Holy Communion has been upon the unity of the church. We hold hands, we pass the peace, we sing "In Christ there is no East nor West, in Him no South nor North, but one great fellowship of love throughout the whole wide earth."

Time after time deep divisions are covered up or artificially mended through the manipulative use of the Lord's Supper. Bitter fights are arbitrarily smoothed over, racial antagonisms covered up in a pretense of unity where there is none. The divisions are too deep, and in resorting to the magical hope in unity without first going and making things right with our sister or brother, we partake unworthily, bringing judgment or damnation upon ourselves (1 Cor. 11:27-29). Making things right involves us in addressing both immediate interpersonal divisions and the struggle to change those structures that create and maintain the divisions. By the pretense of unity and the failure to engage in the struggle to transform our world, we only make matters worse if we come to the Table. In failing to address adequately the alienation among ourselves we seek a placebo and treat the Eucharist as magic.

The same is often the case in the matter of prayer. We ask for what we want, hoping that by our sincerity, repetition, and the use of correct formulas we will achieve the desired outcome. Rather than Jesus' sober recognition in the Garden of Gethsemane — "nevertheless not my will but thine be done" — we assume or hope that our words will insure the results.

There can be a unity in the Eucharist, as we shall see later, and there are answers to prayer, but in neither case are they the result of our successful manipulation of the forms and rituals. Belief in such guarantees only reinforces the broader society's hope in magic as a solution to our alienation.

Nowhere is this reliance upon magic more pronounced than in the television and radio preachers who abound. Send for the healing handkerchief, put your name on the prayer chain, buy this book, and your life will be transformed; come and be touched and be cured. The outcomes are ours for the asking and the only reason for failing to receive the promised blessing is in our failure to go through the appropriate steps: coming forward, sending money, etc.

The tragedy is that those of us who hope in magic as the solution to the fundamental alienation or our lives will end up as those of Jeremiah's day, carried off by the powers of alienation into an exile far worse than anything we can imagine.

It would be easy to conclude from all that has been said in this chapter that the church is a hopeless supporter of the status quo, capable only of perpetuating false responses to our alienation, in league with an alienating society. But that is not the entire story. There are signs of hope. The church of Jesus Christ is not only a perpetuator of alienation; it is also a community of transformation, a living, vital force for the making at one that which has been separated.

•

Each of these ways of responding to our alienation offers us false promises of deliverance from our condition. But the causes of our alienation run so deep that these responses offer us no essential hope. There are other options, other responses that point to the possibility of overcoming alienation. It is to this that we turn in Part Two.

PART TWO

"From No People to God's People": The Process of Transformation

HERACLITUS, THE ANCIENT GREEK PHILOSOPHER, pointed out that one cannot step into the same stream twice. By the second time, the person has changed and so has the stream. Life is constant change.

The issue concerning us, however, is not simply that of change but of a certain kind of change — what I shall call transformation. Transformation is the radical altering from one state or condition to another: from heat to energy, from Saul the enemy of Christianity to Paul the Apostle, from the current order to a New Heaven and Earth, from tears to joy, from death to resurrection, from alienation to reconciliation. The Scriptures refer to what we are calling transformation as conversion, being born again, the year of release or jubilee, and from being "no people" to "God's people." Transformation means fundamental changes in perspectives, behaviors, relationships, and structures that together lead toward wholeness, justice, and reconciliation.

We have seen the pervasiveness and tenacity of alienation and the false responses that exacerbate our condition. And we have seen how the church often unwittingly serves as the ideological handmaiden and practical reinforcer of these false responses, thereby perpetuating the alienation.

The task before us now is to consider how we might go beyond merely coping with our condition of alienation to participating in the transformation toward reconciliation — by reestablishing broken connections, by reuniting what has been separated, by making at one (atonement) what has been divided. In this part the four necessary components or aspects of a process of transformation will be considered and, for each, ways in which the church's theology and practice can serve as an agent of that transforming process.

Any response to alienation that seeks to bring about a fundamental transformation of the situation must be rooted in: (1) a recognition of the incoherence of our world, (2) a new vision, (3) a fundamental conflict with the powers of alienation, and (4) a new way of structuring our lives and our world. We turn now to consider these aspects in the four succeeding chapters.

Chapter 4

"Woe Is Me":
The Recognition of Incoherence

The turning point in the prophet Isaiah's life occurred during that powerfully described experience in the Temple. The nation was at a watershed in its history. King Uzziah had just died after having led his people in a period of peace and prosperity. But now the mounting Assyrian power loomed as a foreboding cloud over Judah's future and the stability temporarily enjoyed under Uzziah was threatened. In that overwhelming vision of Yahweh's holiness, the precariousness of his own and his nation's future became clear. The alienation that had lain hidden to most was unveiled and Isaiah could not resist the compelling call of God to become a prophet to his people.

> And the foundations of the thresholds shook at the voice of him who called, and the house was filled with smoke. And I said: "Woe is me! For I am lost; for I am a man of unclean lips, and I dwell in the midst of a people of unclean lips; for my eyes have seen the King, the Lord of hosts!"...And I heard the voice of the Lord saying, "Whom shall I send, and who will go for us?" Then I said, "Here am I! Send me." And He said, "Go and say to this people: 'Hear and hear, but do not understand; see and see, but do not perceive.' Make the heart of this people fat, and their ears heavy, and shut their eyes; lest they see with their eyes, and hear with their ears, and understand with their hearts and turn and be healed." Then said I, "How long, O Lord?"

And he said, "Until cities lie waste without inhabitant and houses without men, and the land is utterly desolate, and the Lord removes men far away, and the forsaken places are many in the midst of the land." (Isa. 6:4–5, 8–12)

There can be no possibility for transformation until the seriousness of our alienation is faced. We must first recognize the incoherence, the gap that exists between our expectations and reality, our descriptions and the truth, our promises and our delivery, our policies and our actions.[1]

This basic truth is affirmed throughout the Scriptures, which proclaim that for conversion to occur, the recognition involved in repentance must precede. Similarly, the Exodus becomes a possibility only when the enslavement becomes intolerable. Isaiah's experience is fully consonant with the biblical picture of how fundamental transformation occurs.

Edmund Cahn, a social scientist, has observed that concepts of justice arise and laws and institutions that seek justice are created as the result of people's recognition of existing or potential injustices that they want to prevent. In other words, without the recognition of injustice or its threat, there would not arise such a thing as a sense of justice. Justice is a derivative; it follows the recognition of injustice.[2]

In a similar vein, Thomas Kuhn, the philosopher of science, has described the way in which *fundamental* changes in scientific paradigms occur. A paradigm is a conceptual framework, a hypothesis or theory, a model, for explaining the available data. When a paradigm is discovered or developed that reasonably accounts for the phenomena at hand, it is adopted and serves as the working model. These paradigms are, in essence, beliefs about the reality one is handling. Rules are developed that enable one to both order data and to predict future occurrences and relationships. But with the passage of time, new anomalous data are discovered that "violate the paradigm-induced expectations that govern normal science." As long as the anomalies are neither too severe nor too frequent, rule modifications can be made and the paradigm adjusted. But as the anomalies increase both extensively and intensively, it becomes obvious that the old rules are no longer adequately serving. When this occurs, the paradigm itself faces a crisis, and a new one must be discovered and put in its place. This change, which Kuhn calls a scientific "revolution," is generally a long and often painful process, as can be seen in the shift from the Ptolemaic to the Copernican theory of the universe. The basic point here is that the process of developing a new paradigm arises out of the recognition of anomalies or incoherence.[3]

Willie Loman is without hope precisely because he clings to his illusions and denial; he cannot admit the incoherence. His son Biff, who for years has attempted to follow Willie's model, is the one member of the family who has the possibility for redemption because he finally faces who he is and what his life has been.

> I am not a leader of men, Willie, and neither are you. You were never anything but a hard working drummer who landed in the ash can like all the rest of them! I'm one dollar an hour! Do you gather my meaning? I'm not bringing home any prizes any more and you're going to stop waiting for me to bring them home. Pop, I'm nothing! I'm nothing, Pop. Can't you understand that? There is no spite in it any more. I'm just what I am, that's all.[4]

In facing the untruth of the picture of the world that Willie had constructed for himself and his family, Biff became open to a new possibility.

Most of us may be unaware of the paradigms or basic operating assumptions by which we live and would find it difficult to articulate them at will, at least so long as the experience of incoherence is minimal. However, when the incoherence becomes severe enough, we are often forced to become aware of the paradigms. But whether operating out of a conscious or preconscious mode, when things begin to come unglued we are given the opportunity to face squarely what, until then, we had only assumed. As with the Prodigal Son, who could not be restored to his rightful place in the family until he recognized the extremity of his plight, so the possibility of the transformation of our condition is dependent upon our coming to our senses. So long as we avoid the recognition of our incoherence, there is no hope, only continued alienation.

According to Walter Brueggemann, the prophets understood this necessity. He underscores the importance of facing the incoherence when he talks about the prophetic task beginning with critical recognition. Having shown that the dominant consciousness (or paradigm) is one of oppression that seeks to prevent people from achieving freedom, or even full recognition of their bondage, he goes on to claim that "the Royal consciousness leads people to a numbness, especially a numbness about death. It is the task of the prophetic ministry and imagination to bring people to engage their experiences of suffering and death." [5]

Recent developments in theology, most notably those arising out of Latin America, the black church, and the women's movement, have also pointed to the importance of this starting point for transformation. These theologies have emerged from the people's experience of poverty, marginalization, and oppression rather than being inherited from some previous systematic formulations. Because the dominant reality of their lives is the condition of alienation, a recognition of this reality becomes the critical first stage in liberating theological thought and action.

According to Juan Luis Segundo, all theology that hopes to be a resource for liberating the oppressed must begin with "suspicion" (what has been called "the recognition of incoherence"). This suspicion gives rise to questions that are "rich enough, general enough, and basic enough to force us to change our customary conceptions of life, death, knowledge, society, politics, and the world in general."[6] Out of the experience of those struggling from the margins of society comes further support for the importance of beginning with the recognition of our incoherence.

In Part One we noted some of the ways in which a recognition of incoherence, or the full facing of our alienation, is prevented through denial, a sense of inevitability, blaming the victim, inauthentic activism, and hope in magic. What is called for is the kind of coming to our senses that no longer allows these camouflages to function. It seems a modest enough beginning to admit our suspicions. But it is a beginning that has revolutionary potential. Such suspicion is subversive. It begins to erode the power of the anesthesia that has dulled our senses. It is like the first tinges of pain after the operation. The fear of facing the future without the anesthesia tempts us to rely upon it. But we also know that there is no healing if we do not allow the body to begin to function on its own, with the attendant discomfort.

How does this recognition occur? It is quite clear that the awareness of incoherence can arise out of vicarious experience. But while a sympathetic concern for someone else's condition can be real, it may not have the same power as that which arises from our direct experience. Graphic depictions of hunger in Africa may disrupt our way of thinking about the world as a beneficent place, but being robbed at gunpoint gets our attention more seriously. It is precisely because of the primacy of our own experience as the basis for incoherence that the recognition of it develops differently for different people. Hence, no single set of tactics to induce such awareness will work uniformly well with all persons. That is why appeals to conscience and guilt about another person's condition usually produce philanthropy (at best) rather than a real commitment to basic change. If we are serious about transformation, we shall have to discover and help others discover the forms of incoherence that are central to the experience of each of us.

This does not mean that our approach can become simply one of self-interest. What is essential is to discover the interrelationships of our alienations, for then true solidarity can emerge. We need the perspective and critique offered by those who are suffering the most severe forms of alienation, for they often can help us to discover the truth of our own alienation as well as the ways in which we may be instruments of theirs.

As a white male, I was brought up with the expectation that it was my right and obligation to exercise power over those "weaker" than myself: women, children, the poor, people of color. This was couched in humanitarian (and patronizing) language of doing what was best for others. It came as quite a shock to discover that others did not want me to do things for them or to control their lives.

Their challenge to my "sympathy" helped me to discover the alienation such attempts at control caused in their lives, and it revealed to me some hidden truths about my own life. I discovered that the control I exercised over others was only a pseudo power, diverting me from the recognition of my own fundamental powerlessness. When I realized this, I could then make sense out of my father's attempts at superiority. It allowed him an escape from the reality of his own subservience. Further, I discovered that in controlling others, I diminish my own humanity; seeing oneself as in control all the time reduces all relationships to functional ones and eliminates the possibility of true intimacy. Further, it makes life unbearably stressful to feel that you are responsible for everything and everyone. The costs are enormous for both others and for oneself.

The interesting thing about the discovery of incoherence is how it operates on the boundary between empathy and self-discovery. It may begin with an empathic concern for another, but until it moves to see the truth about our own lives, it will result in patronization rather than solidarity. It is when we discover the incoherence that we both share, albeit in different ways, that true solidarity emerges.

Recognition of the incoherence of our own lives or of the lives of others does not come easily. The mechanisms of anesthetization are so many, so powerful, and so subtle, and the recognition of incoherence is sometimes so painful, that we need a space and a community in which we are free to confront ourselves and our world honestly, free to discover the reality of the alienation with which we live. The church can be such a place.

The potential for recognizing our incoherence emerges with some regularity within the life of many congregations. The struggles, disappointments, and hopes, which we often express in prayer; the divisions and fears that we share in counselling; the stories of others who have experienced alienation that we recount in worship; and a theology that talks about sin, sickness, and suffering all offer us a chance for such recognition. While our experience may be largely that of the failure of the church to be such a place, as we indicated in chapter 3, it is not always that way. There are roots of suspicion within our faith tradition that arise both out of our theology and out of our practice as a worshiping community.

The theology taught us through sermons and educational programs has a way of shaping our thinking that can go beyond what we might imagine. The impact may be subtle, mere tinges in comparison to the massive doses of anesthesia we've been receiving, but there is something here that calls for strengthening. We turn now to some of those aspects of congregational doctrine and practice that bear exploration.

Sin

The doctrine of Sin, which can be interpreted in such a way as to lead to fatalism, contains within it the possibility for challenge and suspicion. In claiming that we are totally depraved and that sin is original and affects all humans, Christians have correctly recognized the pervasiveness of sin and its contagious consequences. The Bible speaks of a cosmic evil, a battle being waged between the angels of life and the angels of death, between Satan and God, between the forces of Heaven and the forces of Hell. While the images of that particular cosmology may no longer fully serve us, its power to describe our experience is undeniable.[7]

To say that evil is cosmic and total, involving a life and death battle, does more justice to the seriousness of our condition than the optimistic words of our politicians or "feel-good" preachers. We are put on guard against any claims of ultimacy and purity. There are no quick fixes when we understand the power of evil.

Many of the popularizers of the Social Gospel slipped into the smooth words of optimism because they denied the full power of evil in our world. They were caught up in the Social Darwinian mood of the turn of the century and bought into an optimistic fatalism. Nothing, they thought, would stop them from the perfecting of history.

When the First World War and its madness shattered the glass house of optimism, people were ready for a sober word. It was at that time that Karl Barth's commentary on Romans was published, introducing a new critical perspective. Unfortunately, his corrective was interpreted by many as merely a repetition of the orthodox emphasis on total depravity, which eventually, despite his intention, provided ideological reinforcement for a sense of fatalism.

Between the optimistic fatalism that results from treating sin and evil as less than serious and the pessimistic fatalism that results from treating sin and evil as dooming all human efforts, lies the biblical notion of a tragic evil with which we are called to do battle, and in which our choices and efforts make a real difference. This tradition runs from the rise of Deborah's leadership of Israel against Sisera, the Canaanite king (Judg. 4), to

Paul's admonition to fight against the principalities and powers (Eph. 6).

Recognizing the dominance of evil should not lead us to despair, but rather to suspicion of all explanations and structures in a world that is so alienated. Despair leads nowhere. Suspicion can give rise to new forms. Because we believe in the reality of sin we are a suspicious people. Any Christian who remains unsuspicious of defenses of apartheid, excuses for racism, the arms race, the "place of women," or claims for national security has simply not understood what sin is. While the analysis of what is actually at work and the directions we might take remain debatable, an absence of suspicion is simply incompatible with a serious doctrine of sin.

Christology

Another doctrine of our faith that can lead us to recognition of incoherence is Christology, the doctrine of the person and work of Jesus Christ. Since the church began, it has claimed that Jesus is the full revelation of God's intent for humanity. While the specifics of how this is so have been debated over the centuries, and various formulations have been set forth — e.g., Son of Man, Son of God, Suffering Servant, Moral Example — most Christians would agree that in the man Jesus has been revealed what and who we are called to be. We need not engage in metaphysical speculation as some of the church councils did to explain this claim, nor need we agree about all the specifics of our Christology to realize the enormous gap between what he revealed and our experience. If we take seriously the life and ministry of Jesus, it is clear that the forms of alienation that prevail are diametrically opposed to God's intention. Jesus faced the alienation of his day, rejecting both subservience and superfluousness. In setting his face toward Jerusalem, he resolved to do battle with the dominant forces of the society, both secular and religious, which cast so many of its people into identities and structures of alienation. He neither denied the pain of the alienation that he experienced ("My God, my God, why hast thou forsaken me"), nor did he blame the victims of society ("Woman, where are your accusers?... Neither do I condemn you, go and sin no more"). In rejecting the Zealots' option to violently overthrow Rome he moved beyond sheer activism. In rejecting Satan's offers during the temptation in the wilderness he refused to turn to magic to accomplish his goals.

Jesus embodies God's revelation that alienation need not be the final word if it is recognized, named, and fought. He was one with the oppressed, the downtrodden, and the outcasts. In light of the one whose name we bear how can we remain unsuspicious of the thriving alienation of our time? How can we not be suspicious of contemporary counterparts to Rome and Jerusalem — our laws and moralisms, our politicians and religious leaders, our legal definitions and biblical interpretations, our religious education and the mass media? We are called to a similar suspicion and questioning.

Eschatology

The doctrine of eschatology has the power to help us recognize the incoherence or our world also. Eschatology, or the doctrine of "last things," has frequently been offered as a false hope enabling believers to avoid dealing with the present. But it has the potential for a more radical role.

A New York cab driver, upon discovering that I was a clergyman, asked if I thought these were the last days. My response was, "Sometimes it feels like it, doesn't it?" He agreed and went on to share his literal interpretation of various passages of Scripture, deciphering calendars of the movement of history, and predicting the battle of Armageddon, which would soon occur in Israel. Cynics have and may scoff at such projections, but contained within that perspective is a root of deep suspicion about our present. Why else would someone be so attuned to the possibility of world cataclysm?

The cynics have some historical basis for challenging such views. Over the centuries thousands of people at different times have been swept away by millenarian predictions, some even selling all their possessions and gathering on a mountaintop to await the return of the Messiah. But the expectations proved groundless.

However, the repeated occurrence of such false hopes is cause for sobriety, not for scoffing. If one had a recurring dream, however "unreal" it might seem, we would do well to examine its significance. So too with the eschatological hopes that have been imaged throughout Scripture and history. The kind of hope and fear that these eschatological images evidence arises precisely out of a recognition of our alienated condition. As Pruyser says, "If reality does not first give us grounds for despairing, it cannot give us grounds for hoping: If hoping is a response to tragedy, the individual must have a tragic sense of life out of which hope may be generated."[8] Genuine hope can only arise when despair is also a possibility, when one has suffered and considers the present situation intolerable. It was the heavy load, the lack of freedom to worship, the severity of the taskmasters, that pushed the Hebrews to hope in a new possibility. It was their suffering at the hands of Egypt that led them to hope for a new land that they described as flowing with milk and honey. At various times throughout history people have experienced the "last days," the time when the world as they knew it was coming apart. Europe under Nazism or during the Crimean and First World Wars, Native Americans during our genocidal program of westward expansion, Jews under various occupations and exiles, Africans experiencing the Middle Passage, and the residents of Hiroshima, all lived in the "last days." Apocalyptic images reveal the depth of that alienation.

It is possible to interpret historical events as dropped from the heavens, or to adopt a form of fatalism in which Armageddon is inevitable. But Christian hope is different from either of these. Gabriel Marcel has distinguished between wish, illusion, and hope. Wish has to do with specifics, illusion with unrealities, and hope with a way of living.[9] Biblical hope offers us the vision of a transformation of the condition of alienation and terror. It is the promise of conversion, the claim that the impossible is possible. But such a promise leads us away from the specifics of predictability into a way of living that is open to surprise. Hope is essentially a stance, not a formulated picture of the future. This is what characterizes the creative scientist who refuses to be bound to the existing paradigms and is willing to dream of the possibility of something different, even when there is no new paradigm readily apparent. When we have that kind of openness we are free to face the reality of the anomalies. Hoping and suspicion about the current ordering of things go hand in hand, mutually reinforcing each other.

Our eschatological images and teachings offer us a way to live and look at our world critically. They call us to consider the "last days," the days in which the alienation becomes so severe that we can no longer bury our heads in the sand.

Along with these doctrines that give rise to our suspicion, there are various cultic and pastoral activities that provide the opportunity for people to discover the incoherences of their world. We will consider three: preaching, prayer, and counselling.

Preaching as Truth-Telling

Preaching not only serves to comfort, cajole, teach, exhort, and elicit praise; it also can enable people to become aware of their alienation by telling the truth about their lives. I am not suggesting the all-too-familiar browbeating and castigation of the laity that often characterize preaching, but offering stories that unfold their lives to them.

As mentioned earlier, a certain level of recognition of incoherence can be achieved through vicarious sharing. Telling the stories of others whose lives are starkly and brutally alienated may elicit sympathy and even anger about the way things are. Stories of the Holocaust, or of the starving children of Ethiopia, seldom fail to open the floodgates of sorrow. Unfortunately, the awareness is often short-lived. While these stories elicit emotional responses, our inability to imagine any remedies, our sense of powerlessness, and our desire to avoid pain often lead us to seek escape.

One of the most effective ways of helping people perceive incoherence is to offer them their own stories, stories that might otherwise remain untold. The power of preaching lies in its ability to tell the people's stories in such a way that they recognize the truth of their own condition, whether of their alienation, their power, or their potential.

Such preaching demands that the preacher first of all be a listener. Preachers cannot tell the stories of the people unless they have heard them. And such listening demands exegesis, i.e., critical interpretation. Just as Scripture must be interpreted in order to be faithfully understood, so too must the people's stories.

A method of consciousness-raising among illiterate peasants developed by Brazilian educator Paulo Freire offers some clues for this task. Central to his process is the discovery of what he calls "generative themes." The themes emerge out of conversations with the peasants and are offered back to them in such a way as to enable them to think critically about their lives. Through this process, many for the first time become aware of the causes of their suffering and the possibilities for change. Before working directly with them, an entire team lives with the people for a time, listening and analyzing their words, speech patterns, and lifestyles.

The same is demanded of good preaching. The preacher must live with and carefully hear what people are saying. Few persons in our society have the opportunity for such listening. Pastors, however, have the opportunity to be involved in all aspects of the people's lives from cradle to grave and from work to home, where such listening is possible.

Listening requires enormous discipline, especially for people who have been trained to talk and are accustomed to having others listen. Further, effective listening is done within a certain framework, within a set of commitments. Listening for the sake of transformation entails listening for the pain, the hopes, the fear, and the loneliness that offer clues to people's alienation. Without this intentional focus it is easy to hear only the superficial.

Unfortunately, people tend to talk "religiously" in the presence of clergy, creating a barrier for hearing accurately. No doubt they think that this is what clergy want to hear or all they are capable of hearing. It is critical, therefore, to find ways to engage people in arenas outside the religious sphere, such as work, play, or home, and to learn the languages of these arenas.

The people's stories can then be linked with the biblical stories and the stories of others' alienation in such a way that they can see themselves and their world for what it is and what it can be. The most powerful form of preaching is story and image. This does not minimize the need for analysis, exegesis, and systematic discourse, but these components are background to and building blocks upon the stories and images.

A word of caution. Much of the current emphasis upon storytelling in preaching fosters the false responses to alienation discussed in chapter 3. So many stories from the pulpit are of the Horatio Alger variety: people who make a success of themselves through diligence, resolve, and prayer. Many of these stories are about a select handful who in fact do "succeed," but it is difficult to imagine how such stories would be redemptive for Willie Loman to hear. They would simply reinforce his illusions. No, Willie needs to hear his own story told, however painful, just as King David was forced to face the fact that he was an adulterer and a murderer. The prophet Nathan raised David's indignation by telling him of a rich man who stole from a poor man. When King David demanded justice, the prophet revealed that the story was actually the story of David's own action. In stark simplicity, Nathan broke open the truth of David's world with the words "thou art the man" (2 Samuel 11 and 12). Telling stories that soothe and placate is not enough; the stories must be authentically the people's, which means they must tell the truth about the incoherence.

This is what makes much black preaching so powerful. The preacher tells the people's story corporately in such a way that they can recognize and affirm it. When there is dead silence, one can be relatively sure that it is not the people's story that is being told. Those of us in the "mainline" traditions suffer a distinct disadvantage in this respect and must rely upon other ways to determine whether or not we have captured the truth, usually through nonverbal responses or one-to-one conversations.

The power of the sermon should not be minimized. In our society it is one of the few places where people have the opportunity to hear the truth and to recognize the incoherences of their lives.

Prayer as Groaning

The church I attended as a teenager had Wednesday evening prayer meetings, prayer breakfasts, and special weeks of corporate prayer each year. While many of the prayers seemed endless and an exercise in competitive piousness, occasionally one could not help but be struck by the level of sharing and the risk of revealing deep anguish, loss, or fear that characterized some of those prayers. It was as if that moment offered the opportunity for corporate recognition of the depths of our alienation. Unfortunately, in lifting our burdens to the Lord we usually left them there, floating in the air, seldom dealt with as a community. We missed an incredible opportunity.

The apostle Paul speaks of prayer as groaning and says that the Holy Spirit takes these deep groanings that we cannot even utter and intercedes for us (Rom. 8:26). True prayer is the yearning of our hearts. It is what we long for but frequently cannot or do not articulate. As an alienated people, we groan or long for the reuniting of what has been divided.

It is only natural that such prayer is done in the stillness of one's privacy. But there is a place for corporate prayer that moves to this level. If our corporate prayer never gets beyond the ritualistic recitation of what has been written by those who have gone before us, our times of corporate prayer cannot serve to help us recognize the incoherence. To join in prayer with another is to share our groanings. It may be that most of the time we cannot utter our true prayers so that others may hear. But if we never do, we shall all continue to assume that we are alone in our condition.

Because of the loneliness and privatization that are fostered in our society there are few, if any, places for people to gather and share their true groanings. We are prevented by busy schedules, the competitiveness of relationships, and the opportunities for anesthesia from getting in touch with our groanings, let alone from sharing them with others.

A revival of the prayer meeting, in small groups who know and have come to trust each other, may well provide the opportunity for us to become more aware of the alienation that we share. Prayer is another form of telling one's story. This was beautifully portrayed in *The Color Purple*.[10] Celie, a battered and broken woman who could speak to no one about her life, found the power to tell her story through her prayers. As we listen to her conversation with God we are allowed to touch her pain and, possibly, to get in touch with our own.

We should be free to experiment with forms of prayer. It may not need to be labeled "prayer." It may simply focus upon one person's story or it may be a collect, a collection of the gathered community's concerns. The important thing is that this be a time in which our groanings can be shared. Perhaps corporate prayer can become a vital part of the survival and future of the community of faith, not simply another ritual or another meeting to attend.

Counselling as Unveiling

By the time most people turn to a counselor the situation that has driven them to seek help is usually severe. While some come seeking an excuse, most want help. Although counselling theories and techniques differ as to the amount of direction offered and the role of intervention, every counsellor has the obligation to help the person to see the reality of the situation as clearly as possible.

Most of us don't want to face the truth of our alienation and its causes. But when our pain, confusion, anger, or loss interfere with our ability to function, some are willing to turn for help rather than turn to escape in the false responses. It is at this point that the counselor has a unique opportunity to help people focus and to bring to consciousness those forgotten or denied parts that are at odds with their conscious paradigm or operating style. This uncovering can be a critical stage in the generating of suspicion about the way we understand and do things. Good counselling can be subversive of the alienating social order and definitions.

In order to enable persons to get to the roots of their alienation and to move beyond the false responses, the counsellor must help them to unveil the truth about their lives in all dimensions. This means uncovering and understanding one's history of relationships from earliest days on. It can mean uncovering the unconscious depths revealed through dreams and images. But it also means understanding those relationships in terms of economic, cultural, and political dynamics and how the unconscious has been manipulated and used in maintaining mechanisms of control.

The issue here is whether we succumb to the false choice between changing people through changing society, or changing society through changing people. Most counsellors are adequate at helping to uncover the personal and close interpersonal dynamics. But few probe the economic/political/cultural components that significantly contribute to make us who we are. This limitation is like drilling for decay on one side of the tooth while leaving some on the other side. It is the obverse error of those who believe that there is no appropriate function for counselling, that if we corrected all of the socio-political ills, there would be no need for individuals to turn for psychotherapeutic or psychoanalytic help. Counsellors have a fundamental responsibility to help people understand how the societal means of alienation (identities and structures) are at work in their situation. Counselling is incomplete until it has helped to unveil this level of truth about people's lives.

People enter into counselling already recognizing some level of incoherence, otherwise they wouldn't be there. Among other things, the counselor can help them to extend their suspicions beyond the realm of the purely interpersonal to the institutional and ideological. In that sense, counselling can become a form of politicizing. This does not mean that the counselor functions as a community organizer prepared to enlist the person in some cause. But by helping to unveil the full range of causes of the situation (usually involving basic societal dynamics), the counselor can help a person to think through a full range of responses. For example, how can one hope to deal with a pregnant black teenager without looking into the roots of racism that contribute to a four times higher incidence of teenage pregnancies among blacks than among whites? Or how can one ignore basic economic factors when dealing with an unemployed alcoholic, given the correlation between unemployment and numerous social disorders, including alcoholism? I would suggest that counselling is not completed until it has helped persons analyze the broader social context in which their problem is set, recognize the broader community of support that they need, and explore the kinds of actions they may take with respect to the social dynamics and structures.

Counselling is one of the few places in which we can expect awareness of incoherence to emerge with any regularity. To the extent that this awareness is the first stage in a process of holistic transformation involving both the person and the structures of society, counselling need not be a diversion from the broader transformation. If we are self-conscious about the place and function of counselling, it can be an integral and critical part of the broader transformational process. It is not simply the person who has a problem; the society does as well. It is the recognition of this overall incoherence that the counsellor can enable.

There are undoubtedly other doctrines and practices within the life of the church that can foster the recognition of incoherence. This has merely been suggestive, but it is important for us to recognize that some of our most central and commonly shared religious experiences contain within them the seeds for such recognition. It is our responsibility to explore how we may, in the day-to-day life of our people, take the common experiences of our faith and allow them to become the bearers of the recognition of incoherence.

Chapter 5

"Where There Is No Vision the People Perish": Imagining the Future

Suspicion need not be the last word. Incoherence need not end in despair. As Martin Luther King, Jr., we can begin to live the future. The power of his message was that in the face of jailings, beatings, expulsions, prohibitions, and a legacy of three hundred years of slavery and oppression, he had a dream. While most despaired and others hated, he stood before the world and proclaimed:

> ... in spite of the difficulties and frustrations of the moment I still have a dream.... I have a dream that one day on the red hills of Georgia the sons of former slaves and the sons of former slave owners will be able to sit down together at the table of brotherhood.... I have a dream that my four little children will one day live in a nation where they will not be judged by the color of their skin but by the content of their character.... When we let freedom ring, when we let it ring from every village and hamlet, from every state and every city, we will be able to speed up that day when all God's children, black men and white men, Jews and Gentiles, Protestants and Catholics, will be able to join hands and sing, in the words of the old Negro Spiritual, "Free at last! Free at last! Thank God almighty, we are free at last!"[1]

Anything less than a compelling vision of a reconciled future in which the alienation is overcome will leave us embittered and captive to our false responses. It need not be a perfect blueprint with full detail, indeed it cannot be, but we must have some picture of a new possibility that will not let us go.

It may seem strange to emphasize the necessity for envisioning a new future in a society that continuously bombards and entices us with "newness." But there is a vast difference between the vision of a new future and the "packaging" of the future that characterizes contemporary society. The media and advertising and marketing live by future hype. Everything is represented as the newest. Styles continually change, making what we have outmoded. Unrecognizable differences in next year's automobile are touted as revolutionary. Government and business are overrun with planners. Military battles are simulated on sophisticated computers to project possible options and outcomes. Futurologists hold conventions to lay plans for the next century. But these attempts at the future raise serious questions. Are they not like the soothsayers and diviners of ancient times who project a future that is simply an extension of present assumptions, dynamics, and logic?

Rubem Alves criticizes the nature of most future thinking in a technological society when he speaks of the logic of the dinosaur as leading to its inevitable extinction:

> Power is a simple potentializing factor. It can never go beyond the logic of the structure that generates it. This is why dinosaurs had to die. Their "arrogance of power" entrapped them in the very absurdity of their organic structure. They were thereby made incapable of responding in different ways to the new challenges their environment presented.[2]

This is the dominant logic of our society. In the face of the threat of nuclear annihilation we plan to extend our nuclear capability, building up our arsenal and developing an entirely new arena for weapons in space. In the face of massive inequality between rich and poor we plan a fiscal policy that increases the wealth of the rich in the strange hope that it will trickle down to the poor. In the face of rising energy costs, increased pollution and urban traffic jams, we continue to plan a future dependent upon the automobile. Indeed, what we call future planning is generally an extension of the status quo — only more so.

When we speak of imagining a new future we are not speaking of an extension of the logic and arrangements that have characterized the past and present but rather of a new way of ordering and naming things. We are pointing to a fundamental or radical reshaping that has the ability to alter the structures and means of alienation and to move us toward a reuniting with others, our world, and ourselves. This is what Thomas Kuhn means when he speaks of a paradigm shift.

Copernicus's new theory of the universe was not simply an extension of the old Ptolemaic theory in which the earth was considered to be at the center. Nor was it just a slight modification. Rather, it was a radical new way of thinking about things. There were many refinements in navigation and astronomy made under the Ptolemaic system that attempted to keep the old paradigm functional. But little by little, with the recognition of increasing anomalies, scientists turned to the task of creating a new model. It was Copernicus who imagined a new possibility — putting the sun rather than the earth at the center of the universe; it was an impossible "possibility" from the standpoint of the logic of his day and set things in a totally new frame of reference. The result of his imagination was a revolution in science.

When the Bible talks about the future, it does so in terms that revolutionize the current ordering of things. The promise to the slaves in Egypt was not more straw with which to build bricks for their masters, nor a promise of better living conditions, nor an increase of their rights as slaves. It was a promise of a new land — their own land, flowing with milk and honey, in which they would have their own name, their own leaders — a land filled with justice and mercy. When Jesus had been crucified and buried, the disciples failed to claim the promise of the resurrection because it was such a radical departure from all with which they were familiar. It is always like that with a genuinely new future. When the Bible speaks of God correcting the evils of this world it does so by promising a new heaven and a new earth. That is far different from a mere extension of the logic of the present.

The "realists" always raise a cautionary protest at this point, asking how can we talk about something fundamentally new in the face of the realities of our world. Such thinking to them is "unrealistic," a pie-in-the sky dream akin to the eschatological hopes of so many oppressed people. The "realists" challenge such utopian thought on the basis of its impossibility and the consequent false expectations and useless expenditure of energy that often accompany the false dreams of the deluded.

But visionary thinking need not be about an impossible perfection nor a flight into schizophrenic fantasy. Vision emerges from the need created by the social situation and results in the imagining of a new way of being and doing that, if certain basic changes are made, becomes a possibility. Utopia is not a matter of imagining perfection but rather is bound up with the conviction that things need not remain as they are.[3]

> The so-called realists are wrong on two counts. First, they fail to recognize the power of imagination in the actual creation of the future. As one psychologist has put it, the argument that one needs to be "realistic" (not too hopeful) is literally unsound, since hope refers to the future which is not yet a reality. It is impossible to be realistic about a non-reality. Hope is a subjective state that can strongly influence the realities-to-come; prophecies are often self-fulfilling.[4]

Second, they fail to acknowledge the fact that their rejection of utopian thinking derives from the desire to retain their privileged position. Rather than admit the subversive nature of vision, they denounce it as unrealistic. This is a game played by those in control who do not wish to see things changed. Gustavo Gutiérrez correctly assesses the power of vision, or what he calls utopian thinking, when he notes its three characteristics: it denounces the old order, it leads to concrete action in the present, and it involves the creative use of reason.[5] Such thinking understandably poses a threat to those who strive to maintain the status quo.

Even though the vision of a transformed future posits a dramatic change, it nevertheless has clues within the present. We have all experienced or know of fundamental transformation that has taken place in the face of the most improbable odds, changes that some have labeled as unrealistic dreams. At the personal level we have witnessed the recovery of a hopeless alcoholic, or the male chauvinist who has come to treat women as equals, or the racist who enters the struggle for Civil Rights. Many of us know the power of conversion at work in our lives at a variety of levels. It is not that we have been perfected. We still struggle with our old nature, as Paul says in Romans 7. There is still a war going on within us between the spirit of love and the power of bondage. That is why Alcoholics Anonymous stresses that one is always an alcoholic, either active or recovering. The struggle is always present.

But, along with Paul, we can attest to the amazing grace of God that has given us the victory — not a victory of perfection, but the ability to say no to the power of death and alienation. Would we not claim that our lives and the lives of many we have known have been changed in ways that some might have considered to be impossible?

It is the same with nations and societies as it is with individuals. No revolution, no matter how admirable, can bring perfection to its people, but we would not deny the significance of our own nation's struggle for independence — born first as a dream — and its achievements in the areas of freedom and human rights, however partial. Later in our nation's history the abolition of slavery, for which many had yearned and dared to hope, set us on a new course. Racism remains a cancer within the body politic, but chattel slavery can no longer be its form. Diseases once thought incurable have been conquered, and though new ones emerge, infant mortality has dropped dramatically while life expectancy has risen. To be sure, new diseases, new enslavements, new injustices will arise demanding constant vigil and change. But the constancy of the struggle dare not blind us to the fact that some important changes, however partial, have taken place.

The witness of Scripture, history, and our own experience point to the possibility of new visions being implemented. What we call utopian or visionary is a historical possibility, not simply a neurotic dream born of fantasy and frustration.

Since vision is critical to the process of transformation we must ask ourselves how it arises. Where and in what ways is vision made possible? Are there steps that can be taken to induce or foster envisioning? It is my experience that the congregation contains elements within its practice and theology that are fertile ground for the discovery of a vision in the midst of alienation.

Revelation and Vision

If we succumb to the fatalism and cynicism of the realists we would have to deny revelation, for revelation is a glimpse at life as it truly is and can be. The revelation of God is the height of reality, not an escape from it. What is revealed is the truth about our world, ourselves, and our future.

Biblical revelations or visions are of two kinds, backward-looking (etiological) and forward-looking (eschatological). These visions account for the way things are and the way they are meant to be. The etiological vision (from the Greek meaning a study of causes) looks backward to the roots of our situation. In the Garden of Eden story we have an explanation of why life is struggle and pain and a contrasting vision of what we were created to be. Created for harmony with God, the world, and each other, our pride and over-reaching have caused us to become divided and at odds with our environment and God. The power of an etiological vision is not in the scientific accuracy of its causal explanation, since such explanations necessarily change with the development of science and language. But its power rests in its ability to speak about our lives in a way we experience as true to our condition. We find ourselves both cut off and cast out, longing for fellowship and unity, and also capable of that fellowship. These longings and moments of being at one with another, though transitory, confirm the truth of the image of God portrayed in that account, and the reality of our current experience of alienation confirms the fact of our "fall."

Eschatological visions (from the Greek meaning a study of the last things) look forward to the possibility of our becoming that for which we long or hope. The imagery of the book of Revelation points to a new heaven and a new earth in which the dislocation, despair, and divisions of our lives are lifted. The power of the eschatological vision is not in its ability to predict accurately the specifics of the future, as some dispensationalists have claimed, but in its ability to capture the longings of our hearts that are born out of our experience of alienation and our moments of grace-filled fellowship with each other and our world. It is because we have already known some transforming moments and events that we are assured of the promises of a qualitatively new future that are given shape in the eschatological vision.

Revelation, then, is the unfolding of the truth we already partially know and experience in such a way that it captures our imagination and empowers us to live as we were intended to live. To experience revelation is to be put into a new relationship with the truth that we have already known. It goes beyond our simply knowing to our being transformed by our faith in it. Anyone who has experienced deep love knows the qualitative difference between occasional moments of mutuality and the beauty and power of giving totally to another. Revelation is like that. It moves us from casual knowledge to intimate relationship. In the revelation of God about our intended condition and the promise of new possibilities, we are captured, captivated, and called into a totally new relationship with a truth that we had only glimpsed before. God's revelation shows us the possibility and promise of transformation, and our trust in that revelation becomes the point at which the transformation can occur.[6]

Space and Vision

There are moments and spaces within the life of the faith community in which the revelatory vision has the possibility of being born and deepened. Some of the more central ones are in the release of play, in the depths of dreams, and in the discipline of meditation. These moments of birth have one thing in common: they are unguarded. As a number of studies of imagination and creativity show, it is in the unguarded moments that the breakthroughs most often occur. Harold Rugg, in his classic study of imagination, details case after case of such creative instances.[7] Einstein's discovery of relativity theory, e.g., occurred not at his desk but while bending over a flower in his garden. It was when he let go, momentarily, that the new broke into his consciousness.

The church can be the space in which people are allowed to let go, to let their imagination have free rein, to give permission for revelation. There is no guarantee that genuine revelation will occur (such a guarantee would be magic, like the taking of hallucinogenic drugs to induce an altered state). But being in a place in which space is made for the unexpected has from time to time led to startling visions. The boy Samuel experienced such space while living in the Temple with Eli the priest. There, while he slept, a vision came to him in a dream. While Moses was in voluntary exile in the country of his father-in-law, he stood on a mountain and there encountered God in the burning bush. John, while in exile on Patmos, saw a vision of a new heaven and a new earth. Martin Luther King glimpsed something of the possibilities of a new society while in the Birmingham jail. The church has a tradition of providing space for these ways of being that allow for the breakthrough of a new vision.

Although I have indicated three spaces or moments conducive to revelatory vision — play, meditation, and dreams — only the first two will be considered here. The study of dreams is highly specialized, and the existence of fundamentally different schools of thought makes dealing with the issue problematic, to say the least. Even confining discussion to Jungian and Freudian interpretations of dreams and their possible impact upon the creation of a transforming vision would demand far more space than this volume can afford and far more expertise than the author possesses. Perhaps someone will decide to make a substantive study of the relationship between dreams and fundamental personal and social transformation within the context of the Christian faith community.

Vision and Play

Play is one of the great liberators from the conceptual and emotional limits of the present and to new ways of being and thinking. In play we often discover the totally unexpected. For example, role play and acting have been used successfully to evoke feelings of empathy for the character whose role we've taken, or to discover new ways of dealing with a situation.

Ecstasy is a form of play. It involves us in letting go, in giving free rein to what we are experiencing and feeling, without the controls of "normal" or "adult" life. Many of us have known ecstasy in the experiences of great music or art when we are transported beyond the limits of our controlled responses and are moved to tears or shouts or stunned silence. In these unguarded moments the revelation of a different future sometimes occurs.

I believe that my father, in the ecstasy of a gospel concert at a black Baptist church in Harlem several years ago, heard what Rubem Alves calls "the melody of the future." Most of his experiences in life had contributed to his racism, including a brief membership in the Ku Klux Klan. Though he left that demonic organization many years before, he carried a deep and abiding sense of black inferiority and a readiness to blame blacks for their sufferings and to reject them as personal intimates. To be sure, he had a stated theology that claimed all persons as children of God, and he had cordial relations with some individual blacks. But this was in tension with and subservient to his feelings of mistrust, animosity, and superiority. There in that church, filled with several thousand people, he sat with my mother, my wife, and myself — the only other whites — and listened to the music of his faith being sung joyfully and plaintively by black Christians. As the tears rolled down his cheeks I believe he, like Martin Luther King, saw a new heaven and a new earth, one in which blacks and whites together might be truly free and fully human, in which the dividing walls of hostility had been torn down.

Later he told me of the depths of that experience and of the new meaning that he discovered in some of the songs of his faith. Two years later he voted for Jesse Jackson in the Democratic primary.

Play and the Sacraments

At the center of our worship are the sacraments. These are the dramatic re-enactments of the core elements of our faith, the life, death, and resurrection of Jesus Christ. In both baptism and Eucharist the Christian participates in the very reality to which the drama is pointing and in so doing is carried beyond the limits of time and space in such a way as to be open to the power of God's transforming love.

There is nothing magical here in the sense that going through the motions guarantees a new vision. It is possible to enter into the drama in such a way as to be untouched, just as an actor can go through the motions without becoming the character being played. In fact, Paul tells us that we can do worse than that. Inappropriate participation in the sacramental drama, he says, can further alienate us, causing us to eat and drink to our own destruction. There is no magic in the sacraments.

But there is mystery, the mystery of power being available: the power to see and do things in a new way. That is the significance of the account of the two disciples on the road to Emmaus following Jesus' crucifixion (Luke 24:13–35). Despondently walking along the road, they are joined by a person they don't recognize. He asks them the cause of their sadness and they share the tragic story of Jesus' death. As they walk and talk he shares the Scriptures with them, interpreting the events of his life and the necessity for his death. But, they neither understand nor recognize him. Arriving in the town at dinner time they invite him to join them. As they break bread together their eyes are opened and they recognize him for who he is. From that point on their lives are transformed.

That is the power of the sacraments. Entering into their drama fully is a form of abandon that has the potential for opening our eyes to the truth that is mysterious.

It is interesting that the Roman Catholic church recognizes seven sacraments while Protestantism generally recognizes only two. I believe that we Protestants have impoverished the possibility of vision by our limitation. As Augustine says, a sacrament is a visible sign of an "invisible reality." Just as revelation, the sacraments offer us a glimpse of the longed-for future that stands in marked contrast to our present condition. Sacraments are dramatic (playful) events that — when we participate as little children, i.e., in the spirit of total abandon — have the power to open us to new visions of our world. As the two disciples breaking bread with Jesus in Emmaus, sometimes our eyes are opened.

In some of the so-called non-liturgical churches (Pentecostal and black in particular), the dramatic and playful aspects of worship are expanded beyond the church's officially endorsed sacraments. It is precisely in the often ecstatic, playful moments of music, dance, and tongues that some of the power for a new vision is present. It is an interesting aside that there is a greater consonance between Pentecostalism and Roman Catholicism than is generally suspected, which, I believe, accounts for the rapid increase of Pentecostalism in Roman Catholic Latin America. Pentecostalism is more akin liturgically to Roman Catholicism than to Protestantism, because it is essentially a "sacramental" church in which drama and play are at the center of its worship.

Play, however, can be controlled and manipulated, whether in its ecstatic or its sacramental form. When it is, it becomes magic, a formula to be controlled with guaranteed results. And, those who control the magical formulas then control the persons who desire the outcomes. That is, in part, what the Reformers rebelled against. Their emphasis upon the Word was an attempt to criticize the excesses that had arisen in the Roman Catholic church's control of the sacraments, a control that the clergy used to strengthen their domination over the people. When the institution becomes the bearer of the means of grace — the most desired blessing that the faithful can receive — it has all the power. And this power has often been used for unworthy and self-serving purposes by the church.

When we control play we strip it of its power to give birth to a new vision, which is a gift of the Holy Spirit. Controlled play results only in old visions, visions that reinforce the dominant structures. This kind of control was not limited to the Roman Catholicism of the Middle Ages, of course. It is evident in some of the more apparently less structured churches as well. I have often seen formulas and rituals used to produce intended results: tears, raised hands, shouts, coming to the altar. One has only to watch the orchestrated responses that repeatedly arise at just the right moment in the television churches to become suspicious of the new forms of control being exercised by today's religious magicians.

But appropriate sacramental play, without its excesses and manipulation, can become a space for the emergence of a new vision. In baptism we may see a sign of new life, of rebirth through repentance and discipleship. In the Eucharist we may experience, however imperfectly and temporarily, the unity of those who have been separated. In abandoning ourselves to the drama of the sacraments we glimpse the possibilities of a different future.

Vision and Meditation

The vision of the new is not only born in the abandon of play; it is also nurtured in the discipline of meditation. To meditate is to ponder, to reach the depths of our thoughts and feelings, to hear the "still small voice" that is not found in the excitement of ecstasy but in the absolute silence of our being. Meditation is the time spent digging deeper into the meaning of the vision. It is in meditation that we test, understand, and finally commit ourselves to a new vision. It can keep us from the frivolity of pure fantasy and cheap wishes.

If we look at the process of becoming married we can see something of these two aspects at work. To be genuinely married, the Bible says, involves two people becoming one flesh. Certainly this represents what we have called a transformation, i.e., being altered from one state or condition to the other. It represents a fundamental paradigm shift in which the shaping identity is no longer that of a son or daughter, but that of a husband or wife. Anything less than such a shift in basic orientation leaves us not with a marriage but with two individuals whose identities have not matured beyond their girlhood or boyhood, regardless of their ages.

The transformation to the married state usually begins in the foolhardiness of play, the child like abandon that characterizes romance or "falling in love." We have many phrases that capture the playfulness of loving: "being swept off our feet," "floating on air," "struck by lightning," "losing our heart." In that freedom we see the other in a new way, perhaps even for the first time. The vision of a new possibility is born. But to be truly transformed, to become yoked, or one flesh, requires more than abandon. It requires the commitment of meditation, the careful thought and deepening that alone can sustain the relationship when the first blush of romance has faded.

Meditation and the Word

Vision can be born in the joy of play or the abandon of emotion, but in order for it to be trustworthy, it must undergo the test of time and careful examination. Paul's admonition to his fellow Christians who were being bombarded by numerous claimants of spirit-filled visions was to test the spirits. It is that admonition which is at the core of the Reformed tradition's emphasis upon the Word.

For the Reformers, neither human institutions nor personal subjective experience were the final arbiters of truth. Each was subject to the careful scrutiny and final judgment of the Scriptures. In fact, the emphasis upon the Word was so critical to the Reformers that within my own Presbyterian tradition the distinction between the clergy and the laity is conveyed by the title "teaching elder." Even the sacraments are under the guidance of the Word.

Each experience of the present, each option before us, each way of understanding, enters into dialogue with the inherited witness of Scripture and the theological tradition (the creeds and confessions) and is tested in relationship to that inherited witness. The task of interpreting the meaning of the past in the light of the present is called hermeneutics (from the Greek meaning the science of the interpretation of texts).

The very use of the word "science" offers us a clue to the significant discipline that is required by an emphasis upon the Word. The Psalmist captured it well in stating, "Blessed is the one who delights in the law of the Lord and upon whose law meditates day and night" (Ps. 1:2, author's translation). The testing of vision demands the most rigorous discipline we can bring to bear; the discipline of exegeting both the Scriptures and our own situation.

If meditation is probing to the depths, we cannot accomplish this without enormous effort. Traditionally, of course, the word "meditation" has signified silence and prayer, either alone or in guided form. This is a critical aspect of our testing the vision, of our understanding its depths. But full meditation or pondering adds the discipline of careful analysis to the discipline of prayer. It is this addition of analysis that an emphasis upon the ministry of the Word implies.

No vision of the future can be trusted without corporate study of both Scripture and the current social situation. Both are critical. The worshiping community has the responsibility to become both scriptural and political analysts. This discipline should not be left only to the "experts" but is the task of the entire community in each of its gathered forms. Every congregation can engage in meditation upon the Word in this fuller sense. As Walter Wink has shown, there is a necessary and appropriate role to be played in this task by all Christians.[8] Nor should we leave political analysis only to the "politicians." Reliance upon the experts will leave the control of interpretation and consequent decisions in the hands of a few — a consequence guaranteed to preserve the privileged position of those currently in control and the vision that warrants them. What is called for is a kind of biblical and political populism in which the Bible and the society are returned to the people.

It is this populist development that characterizes the exciting growth and vitality within the Roman Catholic church in Latin America today, which will be described more fully in chapter 7. There average Christians are interpreting Scripture and their own social context, each in the light of the other, with remarkable consequences. Both the church hierarchy and the ruling elites fear the new vision that is emerging, for it directly challenges the identities and structures that have maintained the people in an alienated condition while allowing for the privilege of those in control.

Once alienation is recognized, there is a great temptation to grasp at the most immediate vision of escape. But real transformation demands the time spent in the meditation of prayer and analysis, lest we grasp at a straw. We must not treat the word as some magical formula.

Both the Hebrew and Greek words for "Word" imply a creative process, a relationship that is dependent upon speaker and hearer. To meditate upon the Word is to enter into a careful and sustained process in which patient waiting and silence are as important as action.

The church can be a space in which the discipline of meditation is carried out. But in order for that to be the case, some changes must be made. Many of our worship services have no space for sustained silence. Prayer is often reduced to a litany of talking, with little listening. The discipline of silent listening needs to be recaptured both within our corporate worship as well as within our private lives in order for the insights that can only emerge from such listening to occur.

There has been increasing emphasis within certain traditions upon spiritual discipline, a guided form of meditation that leads the disciple through a process of reading, reflection, prayer, and sometimes confession or counselling. The promise of this process is that it offers a formal discipline for seeking the truth about ourselves, our God, and our world. The danger of it is that its focus too often is upon an interiority that is disconnected from the social structures and dynamics of our world. If spiritual discipline is reduced to a search for piousness (i.e., a feeling of personal purity and faithfulness) and private devotions, it will only reinforce our withdrawal in the form of denial. If it leads us into a thoughtful and sober time of reflection upon our lives, including the political, it can be a major catalyst for envisioning a new way.

We have mentioned that the discipline of meditation includes careful analysis of the Word and the world, or the text and the context. The educational program of the congregation offers a rich opportunity for such meditation. As such, it needs to go beyond either the mindless passing on of tradition by rote, or the reduction of education to a focus on children. We need to utilize the opportunity to teach both children and adults how to think critically about their world and the various visions that compete for their allegiance.

This means, of course, that the curriculum for Christian education must include areas frequently considered taboo, such as politics, economics, and sociology. We need to meditate upon all the visions offered us from whatever sources in order to discern if they are transforming or merely mere sleight of hand to keep things as they are.

These visions come from the Word and the world and all must be tested. While it is possible to separate church and state in terms of their institutional boundaries, it is impossible to separate faith and politics, since each is involved in offering visions. Politics is the public arena of our lives that involves customs, economics, culture, social structures, political parties. All of these are based upon and pass along visions of what life is and can be. Faith and faithfulness must test and claim the vision of a transformed world.

In response to our recognition of the incoherence with which we live, the possibility of a new vision becomes real in the unguarded moments of play that are central to our liturgy and life. When the vision is tested in careful meditation and found to be a solid ground upon which we can stand, then we are called to the next stage in the process of transformation, namely, a struggle against the powers of alienation that seek to prevent the vision from becoming a reality.

Chapter 6

"Crucified, Dead, and Buried":
Conflict as the Mid-Wife
of the Future

When the children of Israel finally had enough of their slavery in Egypt, they entered into a direct conflict with the forces of alienation — the Egyptian rulers who had given them a false identity and imposed structures of oppression. They took the next essential step for overcoming their alienation. Transformation could not occur for them except through their struggle. The demand to "let my people go" was a battle cry raised out of the recognition that God willed that all of creation should live with dignity and in freedom.

Transformation necessitates conflict. This is neither self-evident nor particularly palatable in a myopic society guided by the "power of positive thinking," the politics of consensus, and the culture of sentimental love. It may even appear irresponsible to give such emphasis to conflict in the light of the dreadful crises that are occurring in our world today. Who can bear the thought of more conflict in a world already torn apart? But transformation cannot occur without it.

Even imagining a new future, or envisioning something totally different, is a conflictual action. In imagining a new future we have become alienated from the commonsense explanation for things as they are. The initial step in the affirmation of the future, the imagination of new possibilities, is essentially negative; it calls into question that which is. The conflict with the old has already begun when we dare to envision a new possibility.

The children of Israel's vision of a new land flowing with milk and honey was in conflict with their slave environment that had set the conceptual limits for their existence up to that point. The prophet's vision of a time when nation should not rise up against nation, when humans would beat their swords into plowshares and the lion lie down with the lamb, involves negation of the given warfaring environment as the conceptual limitation for the possibility of the co-existence of the nations. Imagination, or the conceptual negation of the given frame of reference, is the first step in the affirmation of the future.

However, conflict for the sake of transformation cannot be limited to the conceptual challenging of the established patterns of thought, definitions, and concepts. While it must include the conceptual, the creation of a new condition, i.e., a qualitatively new condition, also involves a conflict with those relationships and structures that prohibit the new from emerging. The two central events of a transformed future in the Scriptures — the entrance into Canaan and the resurrection of Jesus Christ — were the result of conflict. The new land and the resurrected body occurred only after the destruction of the old relationships that had defined them up to that point. The destruction of the old came about through the Exodus and the cross. Exodus and cross are inescapable conditions for Canaan and resurrection.

Israel's affirmation of the covenant that promised a new future was only on the basis of a break, a discontinuity from the patterns of existence that were constitutive of the nations around them. Israel's approach to reality was in terms of struggle and discontinuity rather than the assumption of a natural order with an unbroken flow to it, as was the case with most societies of their day. This was expressed both in their actions and in their conceptualization of life. Their distinctive theology set them against the various forms of world understanding of their time.[1]

And that new understanding often meant that the struggle took on actions that were highly conflictual, at times even involving military battle. As Norman Gottwald demonstrates, their political origins were equally conflictual, having been born in the life and death struggle of the subservient and superfluous poor against the rulers of the Canaanite city-states.[2]

Israel's movement toward a future beyond slavery was characterized by a radical "over-againstness," a conflict with the old forms of both their slave status and the nations around them. They refused to adopt an imposed identity and structures as well as the paradigms of the city-states and nations of their day. Both ideologically and militarily they entered into conflict with all that sought to force them into the mold of the dominant societies and religions.

Perhaps nowhere in the Scriptures is this over-againstness so dramatically portrayed as in the contest between Elijah and the prophets of Baal on Mount Carmel. Having challenged them and won, Elijah stood before the people and said, "'Seize the prophets of Baal, let not one of them escape.' And they seized them; and Elijah brought them down to the brook Kishon, and killed them there" (1 Kings 18:40). Elijah was unique only in his extreme, but not in his stance. The prophets constantly inveighed against Israel's falling back upon the old patterns of existence. The temptation to make alliances or to adopt the idolatrous patterns of the nations was warned against over and over again.

Numerous theologians and biblical scholars have affirmed this truth. Jürgen Moltmann emphasizes this when he says that "the prophets saw in judgment that [which] paves the way for something finally new, and as annihilation for the sake of greater perfection."[3] Gerhard von Rad also sees conflict as inescapable: "The message of the prophets has to be termed eschatological whenever it regards the old historic bases of salvation as null and void."[4]

Moving beyond the Exodus, we note that within the prophetic strains of both restoration and apocalyptic is contained the notion of the inevitability of conflict. The restoration that is promised by Isaiah, Jeremiah, and others is the return of Israel to its former glory when the days of exile and desolation shall be ended. But they consistently understood that this restoration could not come about without significant conflict with the nation's enemies (see Ps. 46, 48, and Isa. 40–55).

The apocalyptic strain of prophecy contains an even greater emphasis upon conflict and discontinuity, picturing world cataclysm through fire, flood, famine, and wars. Heavily influenced by the dualism of Persian religions, apocalyptic presses the idea of a definitive end to the existing world and a qualitatively new beginning.

While the prophets do not present us with a unified understanding of either the form and extent of conflict or of the future they envision, there is a common thread weaving throughout: the understanding that the transformation that God wills can occur only through some form of conflict.

At the more personal level, we can understand something of this. To return to the image of marriage, it is mentioned in Scripture that when people marry they leave their father or mother and are joined to their spouse. Jesus used this image of marriage to portray the radicality of conversion that is necessary for salvation. Since he spoke during a time when extended families were the rule and leaving one's parents was not generally accomplished by physical movement, he must have been indicating a shift of a different nature. What Jesus was saying was that when one marries, the old relationship is no longer the primary definer. Where once our definition and identity were bound up with one set of relationships, a new order has been introduced.

Our being is now determined primarily by the new and not by the old. There is still continuity, to be sure. We are still the children of our parents. But now, with new possibilities before us, we must decide whether the primary definition and structure of life shall be the relationship that used to be determinative or a newly formed one.

Discipleship is the same. To emphasize the qualitative shift involved and the conflictual nature of the change, Jesus says that "if anyone comes to me and does not hate his own father and mother, and wife and children and brothers and sisters, and even his own life, he cannot be my disciple" (Luke 14:26). While Jesus was using a common paradoxical form that sounds exaggerated — the word "hate" here means "to love less" — he is emphasizing the conflict with normal priorities that following him requires.

Paul's letters, too, are filled with references to the necessity for conflict with the old order so that the new may come to pass. This is especially evident in the law-gospel debate in which he often speaks of "death to the law." Interestingly, in Romans 7 and elsewhere, Paul couches death to the law and freedom in the gospel in terms directly related to the marriage covenant: "so that you may belong to another."

The central thrust of Scripture is that transformation is accomplished through conflict. Rosenstock-Huessy describes this in terms of the crucialness (i.e, the crucifixional nature) of life. "Man's life must be neither linear nor spiral, but crucial. The future does not stay open automatically, it has to be reopened by your own inward death and renewal."[5] In his monumental work *Out of Revolution* he traces the history of Western civilization through a series of conflicts. The major societal transitions that have taken place are qualitative changes brought about by conflict with the old. The constant emphasis in his writings is that creativity grows out of suffering; birth is preceded by death. "In human history, the break with the past is the condition of any future."[6]

In this context we can begin to understand the incarnation of Jesus. The incarnation is the central revelation of the crucialness of reality. The tension over the two natures of Christ that was debated at the council of Chalcedon is evidence of the church's refusal to collapse reality into a monism, in which continuity prevails, or into a dualism, in which there is no essential continuity. The importance of the refusal to confuse or divide should not be lost. At their core, the early church's debates about Jesus centered on the question of our response and responsibility. Both monism and dualism remove us from fundamental responsibility: monism because all is set, and dualism because the true realm is beyond our reach, influence, or control. The incarnation of Jesus reveals to us that the future comes as a new possibility that is transcendent and at the same time comes through historical acts of conflict.

There are several possible misconceptions about what such conflict implies. First, the discontinuity involved in conflict with the old does not necessarily imply a dispensing with all that has gone before. It is not that we begin anew with some *tabula rasa,* devoid of any past. Rather, it is that the relationships of the past are no longer the paradigms within which one lives out the future or even remembers the past. It is not the totality of past events and relations that is negated, but the frame of reference that is transformed. This is the nature of the discontinuity involved in the affirmation of the marriage relationship — the old frame of reference no longer primarily defines either party. This was the nature of the discontinuity involved in Israel's struggle to be a people; to have a land (Canaan) meant that the old frame of reference (slavery) no longer applied.

Secondly, the conflict with the old ways of defining and structuring involves a discontinuity that is not necessarily dependent upon the amount of time elapsed. Rapidity does not constitute a necessary mark of transformation, even of what we call revolution. There are many stages along the way. The characteristics that determine the radicalness or fundamental depth of a transformation are the element of crisis and a basic change in identity and structure.

Conflict is necessary in the process of transformation because the powers of alienation constantly work to prevent either the introduction of a new future or its implementation. The powers that seek to preserve the alienating past, whether conceptual, spiritual, or material, must be overcome if transformation is to become a reality. The Hebrews had to enter into conflict and overcome their old slave relationship with Egypt before they could become a people. Elijah could tolerate no compromise with the prophets of Baal who represented the powers to conserve the old forms of existence. A man must leave his father and mother and cleave to his wife. The powers of the past do not voluntarily give up their grip. Conflict is inevitable if transformation is to occur.

Once again, there are both doctrines and practices within the life of the church that offer the possibility for helping us to understand and engage in conflict for the sake of transformation. These are the bearers of conflict within our faith. I mention only three: the doctrine of the atonement, the Eucharist, and preaching.

Conflict and the Doctrine of the Atonement

Atonement is the making at-one of what has been separated. The doctrine of the atonement is the church's attempt to understand and articulate the process by which God is at work redeeming a lost people, a people alienated from the basic unity for which they were created. Atonement is the transformation from alienation to reconciliation.

As we have seen, all transformation involves conflict, and fundamental transformation of this nature involves fundamental conflict with the forces of alienation. Such conflict unavoidably results in suffering. But it is a suffering different in nature and for a different purpose from that suffering which is foisted upon us and is for the sake of another's benefit, such as the suffering of slavery. Most suffering is imposed and has no redemptive possibilities. This is the suffering of alienation.

Those who subsist on the margins of survival, those who live in the alleys and subways of our cities, those millions of Africans wrenched from their homeland to become slaves in the United States or economic fodder in South Africa, the Jewish community during the Holocaust, Juan and María in their fourth-floor walk-up, Willie Loman discarded by his employer — all these are forms of imposed suffering born of alienation and ending in alienation. To refer to these sufferings as "a cross to be born" is a sacrilege.

The cross is not imposed, it is chosen. While it is born in alienation, it ends in redemption. When Jesus set his face to go to Jerusalem, he chose to enter into an all-out conflict with the alienating religious and political powers of his day, a conflict that he knew would end in death. Jesus chose to suffer and die so that others might live. Suffering that is chosen for the sake of others, to end the suffering imposed upon them, is redemptive.

Paul describes the atoning intent of the crucifixion of Jesus in his letter to the Colossians, summing up the opening hymn of praise to God with the words, "For in him all the fullness of God was pleased to dwell, and through him to reconcile to himself all things, whether on earth or in heaven, *making peace by the blood of his cross*" (Col. 1:19-20).

For many Christians the above verses and others similar to them imply an end to the conflict. For Karl Barth, the resurrection of Jesus means that the final victory has been won, the outcome of the war has been decisively settled, though there are a few skirmishes being fought by those who have not yet discovered the truth. Many have chosen to interpret the significance of such a claim to mean that we are now removed from the conflict. But such an understanding of the work of Jesus removes us from the essential responsibility for the process of transformation. We find ourselves, once again, in a dualism in which our history has been decided by something done in another history (God's saving history). The blame for such an interpretation does not wholly lie with Barth for, as we have seen, his own commitments emerging out of this understanding of God's sovereign acts were often courageous and riskful. But in a society in which all conflict is considered lamentable and to be avoided at all costs, his emphasis only serves to underscore an ideology of consensus.

Just the opposite is implied, however, later in that same chapter when Paul says, "Now I rejoice in my sufferings for your sake, and in my flesh I complete *that which is lacking in Christ's afflictions,* for the sake of his body, that is the Church..." (Col. 1:24). The crucifixion of Jesus was not an act that removed us from the struggle. It thrusts us into a life of continuing conflict, a life of chosen suffering "for your sake" that is intended to end the imposed suffering.

Redemptive suffering, because it is for the sake of others, is not patient endurance of our lot in life. Redemptive suffering is the result of active engagement in the struggle to transform the world.

There is not to be a once-for-all solution to the reality of alienation, not even by God. What is lacking in Christ's afflictions is precisely the ability of a single event to transform all of history. Such transformation is ongoing and involves continuous decision and action by each person and each generation. What Jesus does is not to bring about a change in world history, but rather to reveal the essential truth of world history, that atonement is possible and that it is an ongoing process that involves constant struggle and suffering, even crucifixion. Jesus reveals this truth by engaging in the struggle of his own day against the priestly caste that dominated Jewish life through an uneasy alliance with the Romans. The consequence of his struggle was death.

Some Christians may see in this a reduction in the centrality and importance of Jesus. They may assume it to be a harking back to the theology of Abelard, who taught that Jesus simply exemplified the appropriate way of life that, if all would follow, would lead to atonement. That is not my intent.

To say that Jesus reveals truth is far different from saying that he serves as an example. To reveal something goes beyond simply setting forth a fact or an idea. Revelation is an act that occurs only in relationship and in the process changes the very nature of the relationship. It is a way of knowing that moves beyond simply accumulating facts to a level of ultimate engagement and vulnerability that leaves nothing the same. The Hebrew Scriptures speak of the act of sexual intercourse in terms of "knowing" another person. There is a mutuality implied in revelation that changes both parties. Karl Marx understood this when he talked about philosophy. "Philosophers have only interpreted the world, in various ways; the point, however, is to change it."[7] A genuinely revelatory experience is one in which understanding and change are inextricably linked. Hence, to know Jesus is not primarily to know about his atoning work, nor to see him as an example to be followed. To know Jesus is to *complete that which is lacking in his afflictions,* through our struggle and sufferings. His afflictions did not end the alienation. The battle is not over.

The completeness of Jesus' action is in its fullness, not in its finality. It is full in what it reveals about the atoning process in world history, and it is full in the deep grounding it offers those who open themselves to that revelation. But it does not end the conflict.

There is nothing magical about conflict. There are no guarantees that engaging in conflict will bring about transformation. It is not simply conflict that is demanded by transformation, but strategically chosen conflict. When we understand that atonement involves our engagement in conflict and struggle for the sake of others, we must then become very concrete about the form that the conflict takes. It is precisely at this point that so much of the disagreement arises among those who wish to see change.

The debate among even the small band of Jesus' followers was largely around the question of strategy, that is, with whom to align, with whom to fight, and the methods of their approach. It is quite possible that the very betrayal of Jesus by Judas was triggered by his disappointment and anger over Jesus' not casting his lot with the Zealots. Jesus' decision to engage in conflict primarily with the priestly caste that controlled the lives of the downtrodden through their alliance with Rome was a strategic one based upon his understanding of the means of alienation and the possibilities of effecting change. Whether or not he was correct remains a debated issue.

If the means of alienation are imposed identities and structures of subservience and superfluousness, then our conflict is with those means in their specific forms today. As delineated in chapter 2, the alienation we experience is rooted in ways of being defined and related that cause us to be either exploited or discarded, depending upon our usefulness to the users. The way of atonement, the restoration to our intended role as co-creators in the journey of life, is through conflict with the *means* of alienation.

In concrete terms this means that we must take back the control that has been lost over the institutions that affect our lives. We must secure the right for an adequate and dignified basis for our livelihood. We must struggle against those who would use us for their benefit, whether for economic gain or political power, status, or otherwise. We must fight all defilement of the earth's eco-structure. And we must seek an end to control and privilege based upon sex, race, age, or nationality. Such a vision involves us in more than mere tinkering with the system or planning within the constraints of "reality." Those who plan changes based on the established logic, whether liberal or conservative, may face resistance, but those who seek changes that attempt to shift the basic identities and structures of relationships will find that the lines often get drawn to the death.

These are the two poles at work in South Africa today. Prime Minister Botha has planned changes for his country in line with the established logic, and as such, his plans fall far short of dealing with the tragic alienation of apartheid. Even the token reforms have met with resistance from the ruling whites. But the African National Congress, which has demanded black freedom, equality, and power, has met with systematic killing. For Botha it has meant a struggle to maintain his political office. For the blacks, it has meant a fight for life.

Those who are now in control (a small minority within that country and an infinitesimal group within the world community) seem intent on resisting, as they have in the past. Because they resist, the struggle will be that much more difficult and the costs will rise. For a church that has avoided conflict at almost all costs, this is a hard word.

There are elements of the church's liturgical life that offer us an opportunity both to clarify our understanding of and deepen our commitment to the redemptive conflict that is essential for transformation. We shall consider two: Eucharist and preaching.

Eucharist as the Taste of Death

We return to the Eucharist, for it is here that the centrality of the crucifixion is dramatized regularly for us. Unfortunately, in much of the Protestantism I have experienced, the reality of crucifixion has been so overshadowed as to have become lost most of the time. We Protestants have prided ourselves on the fact that our cross bears no Jesus hanging upon it. The empty cross, symbolizing resurrection, is the symbol of a triumphant faith. And so it should be. But such triumphalism has too easily led to an optimistic fatalism or to a denial of the seriousness of the struggle, removing us from responsibility because of the inevitability of the victory.

Coupled with this false triumphalism has been an overarching emphasis upon unity. The communion service has become a way of proclaiming our unity in the midst of diversity. But such a proclamation is a far cry from the reality. At best, it is a momentary glimpse of what can and should be. In a world divided, we are offered in the Eucharist a vision of a transformed church and world. At worst, we slip into a shortsightedness that helps us to to avoid the reality of our divisions: of class, race, gender, age, culture, language, power, and theology. Try as we may, most of our pronouncements of unity and community are a fantasy no more real than the soft drink ads that show an international group of youth joined together in extolling the pleasures of oneness and cola. What we pronounce so glibly is not the "real thing" because the powers of alienation remain intact.

It is not that the glimpse of our potential that sometimes occurs around the Table is unreal. This is God's revelation of what is possible and intended and it is the heart of reality. But in the face of alienation, only the recovery of the crucifixion can provide the basis for a true unity. In an alienated world, true unity is the solidarity that is born of chosen suffering in order to end imposed suffering.

Just as John says, "the one who does not love does not know God; for God is love" (1 John 4:8), so we can truly celebrate the Eucharist only if we are in solidarity with those who suffer. Apart from this, we only go through religious motions.

There is nothing magical, there is nothing automatically effective, about sharing the bread and wine. Its efficacy is dependent upon completing in our bodies what is lacking in Christ's afflictions. The magical notion of sacramental efficacy reached its epitome in the Roman Catholic doctrine of *ex opere operato*, which claimed that in spite of the moral character of the priest, the means of grace were made available to the communicant.

This doctrinal affirmation appropriately affirmed the power of God's grace in the Eucharist despite our limits and unfaithfulness. But this notion also served to shore up an embattled institution at a time when some of its priests were behaving scandalously. Once again, magic served as a vehicle for the preservation of established ways.

At the Table we are not offered magic but a very concrete option of completing what is lacking in his afflictions, that is, the opportunity to stand at this time in solidarity with the alienated through entry into the conflict on their behalf. The added blessing to all of this is that because we too suffer alienation, the conflict is for all our sakes.

Eucharist is the place in which we taste the death of Jesus when, apart from the Table, we suffer with him on behalf of others. Until we have eaten and drunk in this manner, all talk of triumph and unity is empty.

Eli Wiesel, in his moving account of life (if it can be called that) in the Nazi concentration camps, tells how the inmates were forced to gather and march past their compatriots who had been publicly executed as an example and warning to the others.

> At a sign from the head of the camp, the Lagerkapo advanced toward the condemned man. Two prisoners helped him in his task — for two plates of soup. The Kapo wanted to bandage the victim's eyes, but he refused.
>
> After a long moment of waiting, the executioner put the rope round his neck. He was on the point of motioning to

his assistants to draw the chair away from the prisoner's feet when the latter cried, in a calm strong voice:

"Long live liberty! A curse upon Germany! A curse...! A cur—"

The executioners had completed their task. A command cleft the air like a word.

"Bare your heads."

Ten thousand prisoners paid their last respects.

"Cover your heads!"

Then the whole camp, block after block, had to march past the hanged man and stare at the dimmed eyes, the lolling tongue of death. The Kapos and heads of each block forced everyone to look him full in the face.

After the march, we were given permission to return to the blocks for our meal.

I remember I found the soup excellent that evening.[8]

Later, Wiesel tells of another public hanging, this time involving three prisoners, including a very young boy, beloved by all who knew him.

The three victims mounted together onto the chairs.

The three necks were placed at the same moment within the nooses.

"Long live liberty!" cried the two adults.

But the child was silent.

"Where is God? Where is He?" someone behind me asked.

At a sign from the head of the camp, the three chairs tipped over.

Total silence throughout the camp. On the horizon, the sun was setting.

"Bare your heads!" yelled the head of the camp. His voice was raucous. We were weeping.

"Cover your heads!"

Then the march past began. The two adults were no longer alive. Their tongues hung swollen, blue tinged. But the third rope was still moving; being so light, the child was still alive....

> For more than a half an hour he stayed there, struggling between life and death, dying in slow agony under our eyes. And we had to look him full in the face. He was still alive when I passed in front of him. His tongue was still red, his eyes were not yet glazed.
> Behind me I heard the same man asking:
> "Where is God now?"
> And I heard a voice within me answer him:
> "Where is He? Here He is — He is hanging here on this gallows...."
> That night the soup tasted of corpses.[9]

In the Eucharist we are indeed offered the gift of communion, but it is only through participation in the struggle against alienation. So long as the bread and wine taste excellent, so long as triumph and unity dominate our response, we have not truly partaken. In a world so alienated, the grace and thanksgiving offered in the Eucharist have true meaning only when the bread and wine taste like corpses, when we know the solidarity of redemption that comes through crucifixion. In Eucharist lie the seeds of conflict.

Preaching as Conflict

Preaching can be a bearer of conflict. The prophetic tradition of both the Hebrew Scriptures and of Jesus is characterized by two things, a vision of the new, and a rejection of all that maintains alienation. The prophets challenged the very foundations of their society and religion.

Richard Shaull has characterized this over-againstness as the "foundation for what we would call today a counter culture."[10] Following the interpretations of Gerhard von Rad and Davie Napier, he goes on to state that "the prophets introduce radical discontinuity as an important positive factor in historical development."

Genuinely prophetic preaching grows out of the same roots as Eucharist — solidarity with the downtrodden, the subservient, and the superfluous. The prophetic word emerges from the situation of alienation. As J. Severino Croatto observes,

The prophets place themselves in confrontation with the power structure, and almost always from within the community or the people. The prophets are never from among power elite; they rise from the grassroots or, at least, speak of the basis of their identification with these bottommost strata. Even when they criticize the people of Israel, they do not do so as power-holders, but by using the single weapon of their word.[11]

In chapter 5 we spoke of preaching as telling the story of those who have been cast out, separated, made low. Prophetic preaching is the voice of the oppressed that has been silenced, but is now made audible. It is the vehicle for the collective voice of the alienated. The prophet is one who has heard the groanings and hopes of the people and who articulates on their behalf. Prophetic preaching is conflictual precisely because it tells the truth of the condition of the alienated and because it points to a vision of a reconciled world that can only be accomplished through a struggle against those persons and structures and identifications that maintain the alienation.

The prophet is the one who withholds the anesthesia from us so that we can no longer remain duped, thinking there is a middle ground by which the alienated can be reconciled while alienating structures and privileges remain. The middle ground avoids conflict at all costs. The middle ground promises everything to everyone, and hence nothing to anyone. When we proclaim the stories and visions of the "least of these, our brothers and sisters," there is no middle ground. The lines are drawn and the conflict becomes inevitable. Such is the source and consequence of prophetic preaching.

This does not mean that our preaching cannot be about love for those who "profit," however temporarily and illusorily, from the alienating arrangements. Those who reside in positions of privilege and power also suffer from alienation, though often without recognizing it. That is because the anesthesia is even more readily available to them than to the outcasts. But as "truth is preached to power," the anesthesia is taken away and the floodgates of conflict are opened. If those who know they are among the outcasts fear to face the prospects of a transformed future, how can we expect those who have received some of the benefits of, and been anesthetized against, the bitter effects of alienating identities and structures to pass easily toward the new?

I do not think we should be unduly preoccupied, however, with this question. The fact is that most of the people to whom we preach, including ourselves, are the Willie Lomans of the world, living with false responses to our alienation that allow us to cope but not to be transformed. We are called to proclaim the truth for ourselves.

Both the envisioning and bringing about of a transformed world are in conflict with the old, a conflict that led Jesus to the cross. There is no way into the future except through conflict. Word and sacrament each are rooted in and give rise to an inevitable battle with the principalities and powers.

But we cannot be content with recognition, envisioning, and conflict. Our souls long for that new day when peace and justice shall roll down like waters, when tears shall be wiped away and sorrow shall be no more, when we shall treat each other as sisters and brothers. Conflict is essential, but it cannot be the last word. In order for transformation to occur the old powers must be dismantled and in their place the new must rise up. It is to the question of building the transformed future that we now turn. How is God's Reign to be realized on earth, as it is in heaven?

Chapter 7

"New Wineskins for New Wine": Institutionalizing the Vision

> And no one puts new wine into old wineskins; if he does, the new wine will burst the skins and it will be spilled, and the skins will be destroyed. But new wine must be put into fresh wineskins. (Luke 5:37, 38)

Recognition of our alienation, envisioning the new, and conflict with the powers of the old are all integral stages in the process of transformation. If we stop at this point, however, we shall be left only with denunciation and empty dreams. This is the limitation of those brilliant critiques of our society by such writers as Ivan Illich and the late William Stringfellow. They provide scathing exposés of the Babylonian captivity in which we are living, and both offer glimpses, if only through their denunciation, of a new possibility. But while their insights are often striking, theirs cannot be the last word. Their function and that of others like them is essential, but it can serve only as a staging for the larger project. We dare not cease our journey here. In order for transformation to occur, the new vision must become institutionalized. This is the task of the construction of the new, the building of God's Reign.

Such a judgment stirs fear among those who have been captivated by the anti-institutionalism of the counterculture movement of the past twenty years. It also causes derision and cynicism among those who have experienced or witnessed the failure of one attempt after the other to construct a more just and humane society or church. For both the anti-institutionalist and the cynic, the basic assumption is that the current order is the way things inevitably will be and there is no point wasting our energies trying to change structures.

For the former group, talk about institutionalization is a cop-out, a capitulation to the logic of the world. For the latter, it is thought to lead to a repetition of the same order, only with different people on top. But despite their disclaimers, institutionalization is inescapable, and new forms are possible. Those who fear all forms of institution and structure fail to realize that they are themselves involved in some form of it. In describing this "Christ against Culture" mentality, H. Richard Niebuhr points out that the mistake generally made by people who attempt to reject any connection between their commitment to Christ and the culture is that they do not recognize that in their very thought forms, speech, and interrelationships they are borrowing from other cultures and creating new ones. Speaking of the history of such attempts, he says,

> When the state has been rejected, the exclusively Christian community has necessarily developed some political organization of its own.... It has sought to maintain internal order, not only generally but in a specific way of life. Prevailing property institutions have been set aside; but something more than the counsel to sell all and give to the poor has been necessary, since men had to eat and be clothed and sheltered even in poverty. Hence ways and means of acquiring and distributing goods were devised, and a new economic culture was established.[1]

Wine must be placed in some kind of a container if it is to be kept and not evaporate or spoil. The choice is either old wineskins or new ones. The anti-institutionalists are simply contemporary idealists who live with the illusion that the more we avoid anything physical or material the more apt we are to remain spiritual or pure. This is a dangerous illusion that either leaves the existing structures in place or any changes in the hands of others.

Some of the resistance to institutionalization is understandable, however, and should give us cause for concern. All too

INSTITUTIONALIZING THE VISION

often we have seen structures develop that, while claiming to be new, are simply repetitions of the past or extensions of the present. Fundamentalists fall into the first trap, liberals and conservatives into the second. Both forms of institutionalizing kill vision and perpetuate alienation.

Fundamentalism's way of institutionalizing is based on the premise that the present ways of ordering things are demonic and must be resisted. Operating out of a "Christ against culture" mentality, they seek to create new responses by borrowing old forms and ideas. In so doing, they fix in concrete institutional forms created for another time and place. We can see a clear example of this in contemporary Islamic fundamentalism and its rigid demand for the institution of the Holy War, as if today's international political and military configuration were similar to that of the Middle Ages. In the United States we have a Protestant fundamentalism that wants to turn the clocks back to a time and lifestyle in which manifest destiny was our operative foreign policy, women's liberation was unheard of, and Protestant religion dominated all values and was the religion of the ruling elite. This last-ditch effort ignores the existence of the Eastern bloc, or the Third World demands for independence, the growing stirring among women and men to end sexism, and the massive immigration of people from other cultures and religions. We cannot return to a time that no longer exists and we cannot re-institute institutions that were created for a former time.

Often on the political left there is a strangely similar kind of fundamentalism that seeks to impose a model borrowed from one situation, with its particular history, culture, and collective psyche, upon all situations. It can work no more for the left than for the right.

Liberals are different. They do not seek a return to some lost past, but rather a continuation of the present course, with some modifications. This grows out of the assumption that the available institutional forms, if led by high-minded persons, can serve the cause of something new. Liberalism essentially is putting the old wine into modified old wineskins, making do by patching up. They want the old skins to hold, the old structures to remain, because they have profited so greatly from them. Because they want the old skins to hold, they assume that they can.

This results in a failure to take the risks associated with genuine transformation.

One can see this failure of nerve in many of the so-called political innovations within our recent history. The Alliance for Progress initiated under John F. Kennedy proclaimed help for the poorer nations of Latin America. But it sought to do so without changing the basic relationship of dependency that was created under colonialism and expanded under neocolonialism. President Johnson's War on Poverty sought to ameliorate poverty within the United States without addressing or changing the fundamental causes of poverty, namely, the ownership of capital and the means of production by a few and the consequent maldistribution of the wealth.

Much of the denominational reorganization that has taken place over the last fifteen years within my own Presbyterian church (and many other denominations as well) seems to have been guided by this liberal mind-set. What we have seen is consolidation in an attempt to avoid risk, rather than the institutionalizing of a creative new vision. In the face of decreasing numbers we merge, citing lofty phrases about unity. In the face of criticism about social action we pull back, citing the need for the recovery of "spirituality." In the face of financial strictures we retrench, citing a need to return to basics and local initiation. I see little evidence of organizing for the sake of transformation. Each change is accompanied with hoopla and theological rationalizations about newness and the future. But these liberal attempts to perpetuate the present cannot pass for the riskful, visionary restructuring for transformation.

Conservatives do not want change or new structures either. Along with the liberals, they believe that the existing forms are working and should be preserved. However, unlike the liberals, they are not deluded into thinking that tinkering is transformation. They have the clarity to avoid pretense in this regard. Perhaps that is, in part, because they share the fundamentalist's distrust of human nature and institutions. However, rather than trying to recapture a lost past, they seek to preserve the current order without pretense of newness. One can see this in the way Reaganomics is proclaimed, not as the imposition of another order of things or a recapturing of a distant past, but as the extension of that which has been at work making America great all along: individual entrepreneurship. What distinguishes liberals and conservatives, within the United States at least, seems to be more in the nuancing than in the basic assumptions about the status quo. Both feel that things are essentially all right. The wineskins are adequate for the wine.

Fundamentalism believes in changing to wineskins that were created for another time and place. Conservatism believes that the existing wineskins are just fine and should be reinforced. Liberalism believes that the existing wineskins are essentially adequate but need some cosmetic changes. The problem is that the old wineskins are inadequate to contain genuinely new wine, so anything less than a fundamentally new structure will prove to be a stopgap measure or a camouflage. Transformation demands new wineskins.

Despite all the legitimate reasons to fear and suspect all forms of institutionalizing, it is an inescapable risk. *Institutionalization is to vision what the incarnation is to redemption.* We dare not fall into a form of heresy known as Manichaeanism, which posited a dualism emphasizing the heavenly, spiritual, and invisible at the expense of the earthly, physical, and visible. The "scandal of particularity" that characterized the Christian claim that a particular Jew, born of a particular family, in a particular time and place, is the Messiah, cannot be avoided. Nor can we avoid the scandal that attends all attempts to give institutional shape to our vision.

If we have a vision of new possibilities, then we must move to the task of creating the structures that can make the vision possible, however imperfectly. We know that transformation of identities, relationships, and structures has occurred historically; vision has been incarnated in form. There are four forms of institutionalizing and they occur at two basic levels, the micro and the macro.

Micro institutional forms are smaller scale, less complex types such as family units, counter-cultural groups, congregations, models, and small organizations. Macro institutional forms are large scale, more complex types such as governments, multinational corporations, denominations, and economic systems. Both levels are critical in bringing transformation. The appropriateness of focusing upon one level or the other has primarily to do with the existing historical conditions. There can be no formula for determining in advance which level of institutionalizing is appropriate at a given moment.

Within these two levels there are at least four basic forms of institutionalizing for transformation: parabolic actions, sects, revolutions, and establishments. Among them there is an escalating dynamic that often leads participants from one to another, though it is possible to remain within just one, or to ignore one or more.

Parabolic Actions

Parabolic actions are attempts to enact truth in such a way as to enable others to see that truth. Just as the parables of Jesus were stories out of common experience illustrating a particular truth, so a parabolic action has as its goal the bringing to light of a better or truer way of approaching life. Such actions are symbols and are not assumed to be the totality of what is needed.

For example, when blacks sat at segregated lunch counters in the south during the days of the Civil Rights movement, they were engaging in a parabolic action. They knew that by that singular act they would not undo all the evils of three hundred years of racist structures. But they also knew that they were giving evidence of a new truth: that the time had come when silent acceptance of second-class treatment would no longer be tolerated. That action awakened millions of blacks and whites to the stirring of a new day. This was a parable in action form.

As with a spoken parable, a parabolic action cannot tell the entire story, nor can it lead to total change. But it is part of the step toward the new. Those who fast for peace do not expect an immediate elimination of arms throughout the world, but they know that increased attention and recognition of the problem will result. Those who voluntarily choose to become poor, as St. Francis, do not expect the immediate inception of a new economic order but they do believe that their action can bring a new hope and dignity to the poor and raise the question of poverty in a new way among those who have some control over its very existence.

Those engaged in parabolic actions believe that faithfulness, not success, is their calling. They believe their task to be the living out this vision as a symbol or parable to the world, to unveil the hidden future. While someday, in the timetable of God, war and poverty shall be ended, they are not called upon to bring in that future but only to point to it.

There are times when nothing else is possible. The prophet Jeremiah believed that his people were living at a time in which no immediate possibilities for restoration existed. There was nothing they could do that would allow them to escape from the grip of exile and be returned to Jerusalem. And so he urged his people to plant trees, build houses, have children, and to seek the welfare of the city in which they were captives (Jer. 29). In so doing they would keep alive the identity of the nation and the hope in restoration. Rubem Alves speaks of this kind of parabolic living as an aperitif of the future.[2]

Alves himself opts for this form of institutionalizing in his Brazilian context. Both *Tomorrow's Child* and his more recent work *What Is Religion?* underscore the centrality of symbol and parable.[3] Living in the midst of enormous repression, he concluded that such is all that is possible at the moment. This does not lead him to resignation but to exploration of how to keep hope alive. He suggests that:

> In the larger sense, captivity is not a time of birth. This is not, therefore, the form that the creative event could be taking in the present. But it can be a time of conception. If ours is not the harvest season, it may well be a time for sowing.... In spite — and because — of the fact that our tall trees have been cut down, our air polluted with fear, and our soil turned into a heap of refuse, a new seed must be planted: the seed of our highest hope.[4]

Certainly his option, as was Jeremiah's, is based upon a political assessment of the possibilities of the moment. Has the *kairos* (the fullness of time) arrived, at which point something more could be accomplished? One may disagree with the political assessment that leads to such a strategy, as many of his Latin American colleagues do, but one cannot argue that such a stance is inauthentic, per se. There are times when nothing more is possible and there are moments in the lives of both groups and individuals when parabolic actions have the power to impact in ways that bring about transformation. There is often a tendency within this approach to emphasize personal lifestyle. The way we live our lives is understood, appropriately, to have an effect upon ourselves and others. For us, it represents an attempt at consistency between our vision and what we are personally able to be within the constraints of the present. With respect to others, it has the symbolic power of pointing the way toward the new and of standing in judgment upon an alienating present.

Sects

There are others who understand the necessity for a new truth but whose concern is not primarily in pointing the way toward the new as it is in withdrawing from the old in order for them to participate in the new themselves. This type of institutional creation has been labeled a sect. Sects are predominantly characterized by withdrawal.

The sect is born out of alienation from the dominant culture or institutions and encompasses the hope for a new future. There are both political and religious sects. Within the church, sects historically have been composed of the outcasts, the downtrodden, or as H. Richard Niebuhr calls them, the "disinherited." Ernst Troeltsch and Niebuhr have each documented the rise and fall of various sects throughout the history of Christianity. The early church, as Niebuhr points out, was a sect, "a religion of the poor, of those who have been denied a stake in contemporary civilization."[5] He goes on to show, in some detail, that the origins of sects are in the economically and socially disinherited people. Those who perceive the dominant society to be essentially the source of their alienation form a counter-culture, either religious or secular, which seeks to live out a different reality. The sect is "in the world, but not of it" (1 John 4). Generally speaking, such communities see their responsibility to be that of being removed from the world, i.e., the dominant cultural, economic, and political forms, in order to maintain the strength of their vision and the purity of their lives.

While some sects eventually become cadres for direct action to overturn the dominant culture, as we shall consider later, the majority remain committed to maintaining separateness and purity, either for their own salvation, or, in rare instances, in the hope of serving as an example to others. Rosemary Radford Ruether describes the monastic attempt to create a paradise in which

> ... the present fallen society is deserted, but in the wilderness an ideal society is formed. Out of the impulse to drop out of the present world, the building of a paradisiacal nature and a higher society is projected.... Nevertheless, the world-negating ethic of utopianism means that one does not move directly against the present evils but challenges them only incidentally in one's movement away from them.... It removes itself from the present and creates an elite, redeemed community where the new age can be glimpsed, but the present world is abandoned to fester. It creates a small sphere of perfection outside the present system but has no message for the city of man which it has abandoned, except perhaps a kind of wistful hope that the elite community may be an earnest example and beachhead of a new world that will become universal at some point of apocalyptic renovation in the future.[6]

Some would take issue with her negative assessment of the limits of such approaches, claiming that at certain times this is all that can be accomplished. It provides the basis for a more extensive action later. But while the rejoinder may be partially correct, there is certainly historical evidence within sectarianism of withdrawal, preciousness, and satisfaction with personal or group purity and righteousness, with little attention paid to the broader culture. Many of the monastic movements, the Amish, the Brudderhof, and others provide examples of this tendency toward micro-institutional concern.

Institutionalization at the micro level is critical, but it is not sufficient. Alternatives, whether in the form of parabolic actions or sects that can criticize or point the way to something new, are important if the problem is one of lack of critique or vision. But when the problems are evident and new directions are imaginable, we face a failure of will. In the face of willful refusal, it is often necessary to move to revolution.

Revolutions

It is out of this recognition that revolutionary movements are often born. Revolution has its roots in the same kind of critique of the existing order, but believes that change of that order, in the form of overthrow and replacement, is possible. The seeds of revolution often lie in the failure of the parabolic actions to move the intransigent structures that dominate and the increasing intolerableness of one's condition. Finally impatient with the kind of waiting that Jeremiah prescribed, or the symbolic actions against war, racism, or other evils that seem to make so little difference, and unwilling to withdraw into a little cocoon of personal righteousness, the revolutionary spirit begins to rise up. The spirit of revolution is committed to changing the basic structures of the society. Throughout the history of the church, numerous Christians have come to engage in revolutionary actions for the sake of transformation. These acts have been of both a violent and non-violent kind.

The Puritan Revolution in England was a socio-political movement for liberation that moved beyond sectarianism, and its roots were based in the Calvinist understanding of covenant. These Calvinists understood themselves as co-creators of history, rather than merely respondents to history. In a society within which forms were thought to exist because of the very nature of life itself, they saw the possibility of creating alternatives. And so they set themselves to the invention of new political forms, not just for themselves as sectarians might do, but for the entire society.[7]

The freedom that was gained by thinking of humans in covenant with God made it possible for them to imagine what the socio-political order might become and they began to conceive of new paradigms for organizing life more cooperatively. With a keen awareness of the incoherence between their vision of God's Reign and the realities of their society, and a firm desire to find new modes of existence, the Puritans initiated several changes with structural implications.

They viewed the practice of religion in a way that led them to self-government. Since they were convinced of the sinfulness of all people, the Saints bound themselves together in a "close system of watchfulness,"[8] which, when applied to politics, took the form of self-government with checks and balances. Second, those who would not accept the discipline of work and faith were subjected to the exceedingly repressive "secular power and controlled violence of the state."[9] Since the ones to govern lived disciplined lives, it followed that the rulers of the states should be the godly or the Saints. Thus, the Puritans looked forward to the establishment of a holy Commonwealth in England. Such a vision led them to political activism, to the attempt to create a new paradigm for the social order.

However, the attempt to create a state in which the Saints were the governors inevitably led to a crisis. Those whose power and privilege were threatened understandably resisted. But so too did many who failed to recognize the severity of the incoherence or who did not share the ideological base for the creation of a new order that the Puritans had in their theological heritage. Despite this resistance, rather than being content with creating a sectarian parallel in which their new vision could be implemented, the Puritans chose to force the issue, leading to a violent contest with those in control.

We see something of the same in the intermittent slave revolts rooted in the black church. From time to time leaders such as Denmark Vesey, David Walker, and Nat Turner arose, calling for the slaves to revolt against their condition. This willingness to challenge directly and to demand fundamental social change, coupled with the ethics of non-violence, provided the basis for the ministry of the late Martin Luther King, Jr. In each of these cases, the gospel vision, the dream of a reconciled heaven and earth, led them and their followers into a form of revolution that attempted to create a new institutional shape.

Revolution, as a response to faith, can become captive to its own rigid ideology and fall into the trap of becoming like the former condition. Gustavo Gutiérrez, warning against politico-religious messianism, says:

> They also ran the risk — notwithstanding the intentions of the initiators — of "baptizing" and in the long run impeding the revolution and counterviolence, because they furnished an *ad hoc* Christian ideology and ignored the level of political analysis at which these options are in the first instance being exercised.[10]

But this danger can no more delegitimate revolution as an approach to macro level institutionalization than the potential dangers and limitations of parabolic actions and sectarianism make them illegitimate. The issue here is not one of discovering *the* way of institutionalizing the vision as it is of finding a way that is appropriate to the historical circumstances. Further, one should not equate revolution only with its violent form. There have been attempts to substantively change the social order without violence. In modern times, the election of Salvador Allende in Chile was such an instance. The fact that the United States government, in collaboration with United States corporations and military leaders within Chile, violently overthrew the duly elected but revolutionary government points to the difficulty but not the impossibility of revolution without violence. Once again, the vision born of faith must be developed and incarnated in the light of solid political analysis.

Establishments

Revolution, if it is to be complete, involves the establishment of a new order. It goes beyond simple overthrow of the old to the actual displacement of one thing for another. It leads to the final stage in the process of transformation, which is the radical altering from one state to another. Without this final step, revolution ends up as rebellion. Transformation involves the further stage of institutionalizing: the consolidation of the vision into a new order, a new way of relating. This takes the form of an establishment.

The word "establishment" strikes fear into the hearts of most so-called radicals, for it is precisely "the establishment" that has been the source of the problem: it is the established order that is the cause of the alienation, the perpetuator of the false responses, the co-opter of visions, and the antagonist in conflict. Movement to establish a new order is a step fraught with danger because most orders we know are alienating. But just as there can be no progress in science without the shaping of a new paradigm that then serves as the operational framework, so there can be no new future without a new order or establishment.

We have good reason to be cautious, of course. Nations that have developed out of a process of consolidation following an overthrow have sometimes become worse or simply a repetition of what they have displaced. Some of the Eastern bloc socialist governments such as that in Poland have replaced a decadent capitalism with a sterile and uncaring bureaucracy. Denominations and churches that have come into existence as a result of a struggle against the dominant and dominating establishment have frequently become a source of similar alienation for their people. Luther's infamous treatment of the peasants in southern Germany and his alignment with the power of the princes is a notorious case in point.

H. R. Niebuhr points out this common weakness or propensity and the errors that have often accompanied the shift from sect to denomination:

> Rarely does a second generation hold the convictions it has inherited with a fervor equal to that of its fathers.... As generation succeeds generation, the isolation of the community from the world becomes more difficult.... Compromise begins and the ethics of the sect approach the churchly type of morals.... An official clergy, theologically educated and schooled in the refinements of ritual, takes the place of lay leadership; easily imparted creeds are substituted for the difficult enthusiasms of the pioneers.... So the sect becomes a church.[11]

The same is true of many liberation movements. The struggles for freedom that have characterized many of the former colonies of Africa and Latin America have come under severe criticism for the errors and injustices committed during their period of consolidation. Far too many apparent revolutions have been only *coups d'etat,* changes of leadership but not of basic direction, disappointing the vision of hope that so many had.

Even when the consolidation and movement toward establishment actually occur as originally envisioned, they are often rejected. What seems like a rather romantic and tolerable upheaval turns out to go beyond what many of its supporters bargained for. One has only to note the official shifts in United States policy from ally to enemy in the case of Cuba or Nicaragua. We were willing to support a struggle against dictators (whom we had previously supported — Batista in Cuba and Somoza in Nicaragua) whose excesses had come to be seen as a political liability. But when the necessary stage of nation-building occurred, we turned on both of them because they were unwilling to remain vassals of the United States, providing unlimited cheap resources for our agri-businesses and natural resource industries. What we wanted was simply a shift of leaders and some modification of excesses that had been occurring. What they wanted was independence and control over their own affairs. Our approach was liberal, the cleaning up of excesses with no fundamental change in relationships. Their goal was a fundamental transformation that would alter the previous basic relationships and identity.

As a nation, we have been reactionary in the face of all recent revolutions for fear that the shape of the world community that emerges will not allow us to maintain our position of privilege. This is a strange posture for a nation conceived in revolution and betrays a short range perspective of history and a lack of understanding of the basic need for reconciliation. Our fear is that, among other things, we will lose cheap resources, security outposts, and markets for our industrial goods. There is some truth in these fears. However, from a long-range perspective, the world can only be safer and more human when all people gain the same control over their destiny that the United States fought to achieve through its own revolution. Anything short of this will perpetuate the alienation of the peoples of the world. The step to becoming an established institution is resisted at many levels, sometimes even by those who were part of the struggle to give birth to a new vision. Some of the early prophets of Israel warned against the Israelites becoming like the other nations, urging them not to alter their loose tribal structure developed during the early struggle with Canaan. They recognized what a short step it is from the creation of a monarchy to the rise of a privileged class that would turn its back on the nation's originating vision of justice for the poor and egalitarianism. Their fears were painfully accurate as evidenced by the judgments against privilege and injustice brought by such later prophets as Amos and Hosea.

But these judgments against establishments, whether they come from within or without, while always appropriate in their caution, cannot stand for all times and all situations. There are times when the risk of large-scale institutionalization, such as the creating of an establishment, must be taken. It can be argued that Israel's existence was dependent upon some sort of consolidation and whether or not monarchy was the right form remains debatable. Even before the monarchy, the early loose tribal confederation had undergone a significant consolidation through the development of laws, processes of adjudication, military organization for self-defense, a priesthood, and industries. In short, even pre-monarchic Israel had a form of government that bore many of the marks of an establishment rather than simply that of a counter-cultural group.

Further, some of the later prophets, in describing Israel's future restoration, pointed to a renewed monarchy (though it was to be carefully circumscribed by the nation's originating vision of egalitarianism and justice for all, with special care for the poor). To deny Israel's need for institutionalizing at the macro level — as a nation rather than as a loose tribal confederation — is to fall into a romanticism about both its early tribal form and its promised future. The danger of a relapse, of becoming like the nations and losing its egalitarian origins, was all too real but so too was the temptation to become a precious group such as the Essenes.

Likewise the church, which Niebuhr correctly criticizes for its capitulation to class and national interests and the dominant values of the society, has at times been a critical institution in the process of transformation. The story is not only one of unfaithfulness. The church in its various denominational forms has been a major player in numerous struggles for justice. It has not always been "like the nations." We have only to remember the church's role in the Abolitionist movement, the confrontation over the war in Vietnam, the Civil Rights movement, or the fight against apartheid. Of course we can find ambivalences, mixed motives, and divisive voices with respect to these stands, but purity is not the issue. The fact is that the church, in the form of large, complex denominations, has functioned at times as a macro institution working to break down the dividing walls of hostility, to challenge the fundamental structures of alienation. Sadly, it has not been the prevailing stance, but it has occurred.

Nationalism likewise has occasionally served as a necessary and constructive element within the process of transformation.

Without having to agree with all actions taken by the Sandinistas since their overthrow of Nicaragua's butcher dictator, Anastasio Somoza, it is clear that the simple overthrow of Somoza would have been insufficient. To sweep the house clean of that demon would only have left the country open to the invasion of seven more powerful demons, unless they turned to the arduous task of nation-building. No tiny country could long survive today in the face of competing world power blocs and neo-colonial economic structures without some centralizing of its economy, military, and politics. A revolution is not complete with overthrow. That is only the beginning. Self-determination for the Nicaraguans demands attention to all the institutional complexities of nationhood.

The point here is not to deny the critiques and cautions of Niebuhr, the prophets, Stringfellow, and others. These cautions are painfully accurate but they are not the only or final word. We live in a world that demands institutional shape be given to vision, a demand that forces us to live with the tension between micro and macro forms of creating the future.

It is at the point of this tension between micro and macro that one of the most promising developments in modern church history is taking place. The base ecclesial communities, or basic Christian communities, of Latin America are a relatively new phenomenon that parallels in many ways the earliest Reformation efforts of the common people to make the Scriptures, liturgy, and mission of the church their own. But while these earlier efforts were quickly co-opted or snuffed out by the development of a new Protestant establishment, the base communities of Latin America have become a driving force within the life of the church and society in a way that promises a new possibility.

Richard Shaull has captured the essence of their form and substance. He shows how these new forms of the church create the space for the recognition of incoherence, the envisioning of new possibilities, the conflict with the powers of alienation, and experimentation with new social forms. The base communities are at one and the same time religious, social, and political, encompassing the various stages essential for a process of transformation. It begins with critical awareness and new vision.

But the most revolutionary thing that is happening in these circles is the radical change that is occurring in the way the poor look at themselves and their world. As they read the gospel and discuss it and pray together, they come to think of themselves as persons of worth.... The power of the gospel working in the life of the community breaks the grip of internalized oppression, which led them to believe that they were inferior beings and thus kept them down.... And as this burden is lifted from them, the fires of hope are kindled and they show amazing courage even in the face of violent repression.[12]

And it moves to the building of new forms based on the vision:

What is happening here is that a new form of social organization is in the process of creation, and as this happens, the poor are winning for themselves an authentic place in society for the first time in history. More than this, the poor themselves are creating a model for future society.[13]

But they do not stop with mere model building. They are moving beyond to macro levels of change.

This vital religious movement is fast becoming the most powerful *political force working for change in Latin America*.... They soon find themselves involved in creating a new social order locally, at the grassroots, and thus participating in a new experiment in popular democracy.[14]

In some countries, such as Guatemala, these basic Christian communities are limited to parabolic actions and the provision of mutual support in the midst of a closed society that threatens the very survival of those who raise their voice in protest or propose alternative directions. Like Jeremiah they are trying to keep the vision alive until the possibilities for creating a new order are ripe.

In other countries, such as Nicaragua, the basic Christian communities have become central to the construction of a new future. As Fr. Miguel D'Escoto said, "Many Nicaraguan Christians have learned that one cannot really believe without fighting for justice. Thus there is constantly born a church that rises up from its faith and hope in the poor."[15]

I was privileged to glimpse something of this reality first hand during the summer of 1984 when fourteen of us from North America spent several days in Escambray, a tiny Nicaraguan village about one-half mile from the Honduran border. About two hundred and fifty people live in Escambray, half adults, half children, all poor. Their primary livelihood is a coffee cooperative that they operate, though there are also some small private cottage industries such as pig-raising. The village is under constant threat of invasion from the contras, whose bases are just across the border in Honduras. Many of the residents have lost loved ones or suffered and witnessed unspeakable torture. The geographical center of the village is a bomb shelter. Next to it is a school house. All males from the age of fourteen years and up bear arms and each takes his turn standing guard around the periphery of the village. Most of the coffee harvesting is done by the women since the men must guard the village twenty-four hours a day. It is a community under siege.

Yet in the midst of threat we discovered a strong hope for the future, a joy in living, a sense of worth and dignity, and a mutuality of caring that was remarkable.

Our country's administration portrays these folks as Marxist-Leninists. But they are nothing of the sort. They are mostly devout Roman Catholic Christians for whom the gospel is a living reality and whose faith has led them to heroic support of a revolution and the building of a new nation.

One evening, at dusk, we gathered in the small school house for a service of the Word, a worship service built around Scripture reading, interpretation, prayer, and singing. It was being led by two delegates of the Word, a male and female lay leadership team that had been trained by a nearby priest. Earlier that afternoon I had watched as Manuel, one of the lay leaders, practiced reading the Scripture passage. He read each syllable painstakingly, making sure he understood what he was reading, and was articulating it correctly. Just two years before he had been illiterate, but had been taught to read through the government's literacy training program.

There in a tiny room designed to hold approximately twenty-five children at desks, we crowded one hundred and fifty people.

There were dogs running between our legs, little children crawling on the floor and onto our laps, mothers nursing infants, men holding their rifles at rest. Manuel removed his rifle from his shoulder as the service began. Eva began with prayer. We sang. It had finally grown dark and the room was lit with a solitary candle that Eva held while Manuel read from the Gospel of Matthew.

> Behold, I send you out as sheep in the midst of wolves; so be wise as serpents and innocent as doves. Beware of men; for they will deliver you up to councils, and flog you in their synagogues, and you will be dragged before governors and kings for my sake, to bear testimony before them and the Gentiles. When they deliver you up, do not be anxious how you are to speak or what you are to say; for what you are to say will be given to you in that hour; for it is not you who speak, but the Spirit of your Father speaking through you. Brother will deliver up brother to death, and the father against his child, and children will rise up against parents and have them put to death; and you will be hated by all for my name's sake. But he who endures to the end will be saved. When they persecute you in one town, flee to the next; for truly I say to you, you will not have gone through all other towns of Israel, before the Son of man comes. (Matt. 10:16–23)

There in the dark, with tracer bullets visible across the mountains just a half-mile away, those simple peasants spoke of the threat that shadowed their every step: family disruption, death, delivery before contra tribunals. But they also spoke of the power of the Spirit that enabled them to both speak and live the truth and of their commitment to building a free Nicaragua that would bring justice to all its people. We closed with the Lord's prayer, a moment I shall never forget. Tears streamed down my face as I barely got out the words that for these peasants meant more than anything I had dared to hope in my comfort and timidity, "Thy Kingdom come, thy will be done, on earth as it is in heaven." For them, there was no division of worlds. Transformation meant kingdom-building through nation-building. As the service ended, Manuel placed the Bible on the table and put his gun over his shoulder. He had guard duty that night.

In the prayers, hymns, Scripture reading, and interpretation, we witnessed a hope born of struggle, a faith rooted in the God of the resurrection, and a commitment to evangelization and social transformation. These are a people who know the importance of institutionalizing the vision both within their small village and within their nation. They know the necessity for creating new wineskins to contain the new wine that is being so fragilely born in that society.

Epilogue

"Thy Kingdom Come": Perfection or Approximation?

Having said all this, we are forced to ask ourselves whether what we have been describing is really possible. Have we been engaging in wistful fantasies, pipe dreams born of our frustration? Two thousand years ago the early church eagerly anticipated the imminent coming of the Reign of God that would be ushered in by the return of Christ and would eventuate in the redress of injustice, restoration of lost dignity, healing of wounds, setting free of captives, and reconciliation of the alienated. But these expectations largely have remained unfulfilled to this day. Are we simply repeating the folly of various dreamers throughout the ages who have gathered expectantly on mountaintops to await the return of the Messiah, only to see their hopes dashed? Will the new age ever be ushered in?

The soup tastes like corpses for most of the world's people. Only mindless optimism can blind us to the enormity of the powers of alienation in an age that has suffered the atrocities of the Holocaust, South African apartheid, brutal dictatorships, starvation of millions, terrorism, and threat of nuclear annihilation. Daily, we are marched to the parade grounds to witness the execution of the innocent and our hearts cry out, "Where is God now?"

There can be no escaping the difficulty posed by the contrast of a vision that is cosmic, absolute, and final, with institutional forms that are particular, limited, and transient. How do we understand what we are doing to be the work of God's Reign when the successes are so few and the odds are so heavily stacked against us?

How are we to understand the possibility and reality of God's Reign in our world? It cannot be a purely inward or future event. God's Reign is neither simply that which occurs within our hearts, nor is it a metaphysical reality that occurs outside of history in some distant time and place. According to Jesus, it is among us or in our midst, it is fulfilled this day, and it is to be on earth, as it is in heaven.

There is no single biblical image or understanding of God's Reign. George Pixley describes the various ways in which the Reign of God has been given shape throughout the Scriptures and concludes that there is no Reign of God in the abstract. It is always pictured in relation to something quite concrete. "The idea has no existence in its purity as an abstraction. It must always find expression in some particular historical project."[1] At times these historical embodiments of the notion were used to perpetuate the power and privilege of the ruling classes, at other times to set in motion the liberation of the oppressed. In other words, the Reign of God in the Bible is always related to concrete historical realities and has been used as both an instrument of alienation and a source of vision for a transformed future.

As alienating, the notion of God's Reign emphasized either a fixed revelation which supplied legalistic structures for a hierarchical and stratified social order such as King Solomon's dynasty, or a privatized message of escape through purely internal or future change that was offered to the suffering as a coping mechanism. God's Reign offered them "private dreams to compensate for an intolerable public reality."[2]

As transforming, the notion of God's Reign focused on conflict with the old and a vision of something entirely different in this world, as seen in the historical formation of early Israel as it struggled against the Canaanite city states, and in Jesus' actions on behalf of "justice and freedom for the working people of Palestine."[3] The Reign of God, understood as the source of transformation in the face of alienation, is historical, i.e., it always comes in the shape of concrete political options available at a given time.

This emphasis upon the Reign of God as historical, rather

than as simply internal or in some future eternity, has implications for what we can expect in our struggle for transformation. At bottom it means that God's Reign, as an historical reality, cannot be perfect.

Perfection is not the claim made by Jesus about the God's Reign. Certainly when he said that God's Reign is among us, already present, he was not describing a perfect situation. The powers of alienation were rampant. Jesus' pronouncement of God's Reign had to contend with a religious and political hierarchy that sought to maintain its privileged status at the expense of the poor. The contention finally led to his crucifixion.

Nor can the claim of perfection or perfectability be made after the crucifixion and resurrection. The powers of darkness are still strong. If Jesus' atoning work on the cross and his resurrection did not bring about the perfect world, the new heaven and the new earth, then how can we expect our efforts and struggles in his name to have any greater effect?

Some Latin American liberation theologians have offered us a way of understanding the Reign of God in terms that they call a "historical project." As Lucio Gera says, a historical project involves a "definite particular option for the Church. It has to decide in favor of a given system at a given time and support it. Therefore the Church participates in politics. It may make the wrong choice, to be sure, but it cannot avoid making one."[4] He goes on to reject the notion of a theocratic state in which the church has control over the political realm but at the same time underscores the necessity of opting for some political form.

A historical project is time limited, never perfect, and always subject to criticism. But it also is that which appears as the most promising way ahead, given our analysis of the current conditions.

Most of us don't find it terribly difficult to accept something of this approach at the level of personal ethics. Dietrich Bonhoeffer, discussing truth telling, poses the dilemma of a young school lad being asked by his teacher in front of the class if his father gets drunk. Embarrassed, the boy denies the truth. Bonhoeffer defends the boy, citing the inappropriateness of the teacher's public probing and the limited options available to him.[5]

Historical projects are interim political choices available in concrete historical circumstances. They constitute the structural or political level of interim ethics. As such, they are never perfect or complete, but they are necessary and can be life giving.

In the light of this understanding, we are free to give ourselves to the task of transformation beginning with confession and denunciation, moving to envisioning, entering into conflict with the forces of alienation, and creating new historical structures that will embody the vision.

Just as the historical project is historically conditioned and limited, so too is its originating vision. It is constantly unfolding, as the Spirit of God enables us in faith to see our alienating circumstances clearly and to imagine a more human possibility. It is born out of the experience of being no people and it is nurtured in the dialogue with those who now have a new name. In the light of this, each people, each generation in each place is called upon to specify the vision by which it operates and the historical project to which that vision is leading them.

There is ample evidence of the historically changing nature of political projects within the Scriptures. Gideon, Deborah, and others of the Judges understood their task to be the destruction of the enemy forces. Moses led his people in a flight from slavery. Jeremiah counselled the captives to plant trees, build houses, have children, and pray for the Shalom of the city in which they were held captive. The Apostle Paul urged obedience to the authorities in Rome. In four distinctly different circumstances God's people were called upon to engage in four distinctly different political choices.

Both the vision and the historical project must emerge out of careful study of the Scriptures, prayer, and political analysis; all in dialogue with others, especially the poor. In trying to hear the Word of God for our time through this dialogue with others, both in the United States and throughout the Third World, I have come to some tentative conclusions about the shape of the Reign of God and the historical project for our society that is necessary to approximate the vision. It is impossible, short of another book, to expand fully upon what follows. But in the spirit of trying to end our brokenness, I offer it as part of the ongoing struggle to "prepare the way of the Lord."

The Vision of God's Reign

1. *The Provision of Basic Material Needs for All People.* Everyone shall have sufficient to meet the needs of a nutritious diet, adequate and affordable housing, and quality health care of both a preventative and acute type.

2. *Ecological Wholeness.* The community of which we are a part includes the entire natural world and we must order our lives in such a way that planning, resource usage, production, and consumption are based upon the recognition of the interrelatedness of all of life.

3. *Celebration of Life.* We need to affirm the totality of our humanity, the affective as well as the rational, play as well as work, culture as well as science, imagination as well as pragmatism. Worship and celebration shall be at the center of our lives.

4. *Meaningful Work.* All persons shall be given opportunity to make a contribution to the society and to express themselves through creative work. While it may not be possible to avoid non-creative work, no one should be relegated only to that and deprived of the accomplishments and satisfaction of good labor. All should share in the burden of the non-creative aspects.

5. *Life-Long Education.* The opportunity for all forms of continuing education — technical training, aesthetics, theory, and personal growth — shall be available to everyone for the sake of their ongoing development.

6. *Maximum Participation in Decision-Making.* All persons shall have the right and the means to participate in the decisions that affect their lives and in which they choose to participate. The decision to grant that authority to someone else needs to be non-coerced and based on a coincidence of values. Further, a means of recalling such authority shall be built into the decision-making structures.

7. *Cooperative Interdependence.* Self-determination must be held in tension with the achievement of collective

values. Genuine individuality should be fostered, but in such a way that mutuality and cooperation are possible.

8. *Pluralism.* We should enjoy and encourage a diversity of values, cultural forms, and lifestyles for the richness that can result from their interaction. No differences, e.g., of race, sex or age, should be seen as a reason for alleged superiority or a hierarchy of power. All forms of diversity should be encouraged so long as they do not exploit, injure, or prohibit others from the fullness of their lives.

9. *Openness to the Future.* All structures and laws need to allow for the possibility of growth and change. We need structures that evolve as open systems, allowing for continuous questioning, critique, and reshaping. Freedom of speech, access to information, due process, and forums for debate and discussion shall be available at the local, national, and international levels.

The Historical Project

If we affirm these components of the vision of a transformed society, we are constantly forced to make priority decisions that place one in tension with the others. This does not mean that one is less important or can be given up, only that the historical project demanded at this moment, as best we can determine, calls for certain aspects of the vision to be more critical for the time being. Sometimes the choices will be difficult.

The question of priorities cannot be decided in the abstract or in advance. That is why borrowing a historical project developed elsewhere is a dead end. Rather, the situation demands a thorough wrestling with the implications of each choice. While we should be inherently uncomfortable with any narrowing of our scope of action, and the scope of our overall vision dare never be narrowed, we cannot escape the choices that come with approximation.

Given all this, I have come to the conclusion that we must begin to face the limits of capitalism as it has been developed in our Western society and to explore options that begin to move us toward a more democratic economic structure as well as a more democratic political structure. The fundamental means of alienation in this society are related to capitalism. So much of the using, being used, or uselessness as seen in chapter 2 are directly tied in with the issue of who owns, who controls, and who decides. It is a question of power. The elderly, the poor, the sick, the workers, all lack fundamental power to shape their lives in line with the vision we have set forth. So long as decisions are made for the sake of the profit of a few or even for a significant number but not for all, we will remain alienated. The nature of our alienation is linked to our dominant form of social organization, capitalism.

This does not mean that other societal forms are perfect. It is rather a judgment upon the structures within which we are living. The prophetic task is appropriately addressed to ourselves, to our own nation, structures, and people. We bear the responsibility to seek the transformation of our society in line with the vision of the Reign that God has revealed to us.

If this analysis is correct, then the historical project facing us in the United States is a form of democratic socialism (economic and political democracy) that incorporates as much of the vision as possible. An economic and political democracy would be new in our Western society. While we have a form of *political* democracy, the absence of an *economic* democracy leaves the basic control over all of life, including the political arena, in the hands of those who control the economy.

Any clues we have from other experiments are only clues, not blueprints. That is for two reasons. First, there is no existing model of a truly democratic socialism. Much of what has been passed off as socialism has rather been a form of totalitarian control — often forced upon the society by the reluctance of those formerly in control to allow for a new direction. The ones who have lost control — whether the former internal oligarchy or the imperial powers from outside — consistently have created havoc for the new leadership. This was true of Batista's followers in Cuba and is true of the Somocistas today in Nicaragua. And in both cases the United States played a leading role in trying to turn back the clock. In the face of such enormous threats it is little wonder that consolidation has taken such a turn. What is amazing is that things are not worse. Second, a truly indigenous form of democratic socialism cannot be borrowed from elsewhere, because our nation has its own distinctive history, psychology, and culture. It cannot be imposed or borrowed but must be created from within and, as such, it will have its own peculiar shape and characteristics.

The use of the word "socialism," even if coupled with the word "democratic," strikes fear into the hearts of many within our society. In some ways, this is understandable, for we have seen the excesses and failures of attempts that claim that name. But so, too, have we seen the excesses and failures of those who claim the name of capitalism, or even Christianity, yet those failures do not seem to dissuade us from either claiming those heritages or placing our hope in them. We stand at a new point in history and we dare not allow our fears and shibboleths to control our choices. What drives us forward is the vision of God's Reign.

It is proper to ask why we need opt for socialism, and what is meant by that term, since it is so loaded a designation. Democracy demands socialism. That is because socialism, in which control and decision-making over the means of production are placed in the hands of the people, is the economic equivalent of what we mean when we speak of political democracy, in which control and decision-making over the political process are placed in the hands of the people. There are various ways in which political democracy can be played out, for example, representative, multi-party, parliamentary, or town meeting systems. In the same manner there are various ways in which socialism with respect to the economic arena can be played out, with, for example, varying degrees of centralization and differing ways of distributing profits. The point is that where democracy functions authentically, the leaders' agenda is that of the people, however they may have been chosen. So, too, where socialism authentically functions, economic decisions are made by and for the sake of the people. The difference between democracy and fascism is clear. In democracy the people's agenda is central; in fascism, the elite's agenda and interests are served. Similarly, the difference between socialism and capitalism is clear. In socialism, to cite an example, housing is for sheltering people. In capitalism, it is only incidentally for shelter and primarily a vehicle for profiting a few.

It is precisely around such basic issues as food, shelter, health care, energy, and transportation, that the connection between democracy as politics and economics becomes clear. Genuine democracy must be fully participatory and for the sake of the people, not controlled by a few for the sake of a few. In order for this to be the case, it must move beyond "politics" to the entire "polis," which includes the economic arena.

From many of the experiences and illustrations of alienation noted in the first two chapters, it is inescapable that the relationship between users, used, and the useless is not simply an economic one, but pervasively racist and sexist as well. The users are all too frequently white and male, the used and useless all too frequently people of color and women. There is a direct linkage among capitalism, racism, and sexism. Capitalism is not the only economic structure under which the others may appear, but it has proven to fit hand and glove with them and, I would argue, to lead to their increased power, perverseness, and pervasiveness.[6] In taking up the historical project of democratic socialism we are inextricably engaged in struggling against the evils of racism and sexism.

The vision of God's Reign, when coupled with a critique of capitalism and the distinctiveness of our nation's history and culture, leads me to understand the shape of a democratic socialism in terms of a mixed economy, that is, a balance between centralized national and regional controls to insure basic needs, and personal initiative and entrepreneurial opportunities within these guidelines. Wealth distribution would be guided by a combination of persons' needs, contribution to society, and a fixed minimum and maximum that could be achieved in part through certain forms of taxation. While this is far too sketchy for anything other than clues for the direction that I believe to be appropriate, it does provide an opportunity for others to join in the discussion and contribute to the shaping of the historical project.

Neither democracy nor socialism is a panacea. We know that no political or economic structures will be perfect, but we clearly can come much closer to the vision of God's Reign than is now the case. No project will incorporate all aspects of the vision in its totality, but we can strive for greater approximation. The question is whether we choose to remain in our familiar and accustomed condition of alienation or to take the risks of creating the future. Having lived with the alienation produced by a capitalist civilization I am willing to take the risk of democratic socialism as a historical project.

In the final analysis, whatever we do in the face of alienation is a matter of faith — either good faith or bad faith, faith in the powers of life or faith in the powers of death. There is no other option than to trust ourselves either to the continuation of the past and its alienation or to the future and the promise of reconciliation. And faith is a wager. The assurances we have are not guarantees but rather the evidence of the results of power at work in our world, either the power of alienation or the power of transformation. It is our choice as to which evidence we shall give the greatest weight, as to which evidence we shall allow to determine the direction of our wager.

As the people of Elijah's time, we are called upon to make a wager. To paraphrase the choice posed by Elijah, "Why do we limp between two opinions? If transformation is possible, then why do we not affirm and live its stages; but if alienation be the final truth, then let us turn to the false responses that allow us to cope with the inevitable."

Life is nothing more and nothing less than the wager of faith; faith in the finality of death or the power of the resurrection, faith in inevitability or surprise. The result of our wager will determine whether we remain "no people" or become "God's people."

Notes

Chapter 1: "Once You Were No People"

1. Arthur Miller, *Death of a Salesman* (New York: Viking, 1949).
2. *Wall Street Journal*, September 19, 1985.
3. For more information on this see Donald McGavran, *Church Growth: Strategies that Work* (Nashville: Abingdon, 1980), or *How to Grow a Church* (Ventura, Calif.: Regal Books, 1973).
4. See Herbert Marcuse's treatment of the concept of repression and false consciousness in *One Dimensional Man* (Boston: Beacon Press, 1966).
5. The notion of alienation as the starting point for all of Marx's theory is based on the earliest works of Marx, which Erich Fromm interprets in his *Marx's Concept of Man* (New York: Frederick Ungar, 1966). The works of Marx upon which he draws are *The Economic and Philosophic Manuscripts of 1844*, Dirk J. Struik, ed. (New York: International Pub. Co., 1964). See also C. Leroy Gaylord, "The Concept of Alienation: An Attempt at a Definition," in *Marxism and Alienation*, ed. Herbert Aptheker (New York: Humanities Press, 1965).
6. See Antonio Gramsci, *Prison Notebooks: Selections* (New York: International Pub. Co., 1971), and *Selections from Cultural Writing*, ed. Geoffrey Newell-Smith (Cambridge: Harvard University Press, 1985). Also see Leszek Kolakowski, *Toward a Marxist Humanism: Essays on the Left Today* (New York: Grove Press, 1968).
7. Health Policy Advisory Committee, *The American Health Empire: Power, Profits, Politics* (New York: Random, 1971).
8. Jonathan Kozol, *Illiterate America* (New York: Doubleday Anchor, 1985).
9. Dorothee Soelle, *Suffering* (Philadelphia: Fortress, 1975).

Chapter 2: "Bricks without Straw"

1. Alex Haley, *Roots* (Garden City, N.Y.: Doubleday, 1976).
2. Gerhard von Rad, *Old Testament Theology*, vol. 1 (New York: Harper Bros., 1962), p. 2.
3. See the Center for National Policy Review Staff, *The Feminization of Poverty: Women, Work and Welfare* (Washington, D.C.: Center for National Policy Review, 1978).

Chapter 3: "Scattered over the Face of the Earth"

1. S. R. Driver. *The Book of Genesis* (New York: Methuen and Co., 1905), p. 135.
2. Charles T. Fritsch, *Genesis* (Richmond: John Knox, 1959), p. 50.
3. For a fuller discussion of the relationship between fatalism and traditional religions see Arend Th. van Leeuwen, *Christianity in World History* (New York: Charles Scribner's Sons, 1964).
4. See Paulo Freire, *Pedagogy of the Oppressed* (New York: Continuum, 1970), who describes the various ways that illiterate peasants ascribe their politically and economically created condition to a fate beyond human control.
5. The social, political, and economic consequences of Calvinism as it took shape in its historical development after the Reformation are described by Max Weber, *The Protestant Ethic and the Spirit of Capitalism* (New York: Scribner's, 1958), and Michael Walzer, *The Reformation of the Saints* (Cambridge, Mass.: Harvard University Press, 1965).
6. *The Book of Common Prayer,* 1945 edition.
7. Thomas Kuhn, *The Structure of Scientific Revolutions* (Chicago: University of Chicago Press, 1962).
8. *The Encyclopedia of the Social Sciences,* ed. David Sills, vol. 15 (New York: Macmillan and the Free Press, 1968), pp. 618–621.
9. Karl Barth. *Dogmatics in Outline* (London: SCM Press, 1958), p. 122.
10. Karl Barth. *Church Dogmatics,* III/2 (Edinburgh: T. & T. Clark, 1960), p. 490.
11. Karl Barth. *Church Dogmatics,* II/2, (Edinburgh: T. & T. Clark, 1956), p. 66.
12. William Ryan. *Blaming the Victim* (New York: Vintage Books, 1976), p. 13.
13. Ibid., p. 11.
14. Ibid., p. 15.
15. Richard Sennett and Jonathan Cobb, *The Hidden Injuries of Class* (New York: Random House, 1973).
16. Rudolph Otto, *The Idea of the Holy,* 2nd ed. (Oxford: Oxford University Press, 1950).
17. Juan Luis Segundo, *Community Called Church* (Maryknoll, N.Y.: Orbis, 1973), p. 39

Chapter 4: "Woe Is Me"

1. The phrase "recognition of incoherence" is derived from Manfred Halpern, whose seminal work on the theory of transformation was printed in unpublished form in 1980, "Notes on the Theory and Practice of Transformation." His impact on my own thinking has been significant though the stages as set forth here do not attempt to represent the complexity of his approach. Since completing this manuscript I have read David T. Abalos's study *Latinos in the United States: The Sacred and the Political* (Notre Dame: University of Notre Dame Press, 1986), which is based upon Halpern's theory and which summarizes it in lucid fashion. In addition, Abalos offers a groundbreaking vision of empowerment for the Latino community.

2. Edmund Cahn. *The Sense of Injustice* (Bloomington: Indiana University Press, 1964), pp. 13-14.
3. Kuhn, *The Structure of Scientific Revolutions*.
4. Miller, *Death of a Salesman*, p. 32.
5. Walter Brueggemann, *Prophetic Imagination* (Philadelphia: Fortress, 1978), p. 46.
6. Juan Luis Segundo, *The Liberation of Theology* (Maryknoll, N.Y.: Orbis, 1976), p. 8.
7. For a fresh biblical approach to an understanding of the "principalities and powers," see Walter Wink, *Naming the Powers: The Language of Power in the New Testament* (Philadelphia: Fortress, 1984), and *Unmasking the Powers: The Invisible Forces that Determine Human Existence* (Philadelphia: Fortress, 1986).
8. P. W. Pruyser, "Phenomenology and the Dynamics of Hoping," in *The Journal of the Scientific Study of Religion*, vol. 3, p. 92.
9. Gabriel Marcel, *Homo Viator: Introduction to a Metaphysic of Hope* (London: V. Gollancz, 1951).
10. Alice Walker, *The Color Purple* (New York: Washington Square Press, 1983).

Chapter 5: "Where There Is No Vision the People Perish"

1. *A Testament of Hope: The Essential Writings of Martin Luther King, Jr.*, ed. James Melville Washington (New York: Harper & Row, 1986), p. 219.
2. Rubem Alves, *Tomorrow's Child* (New York: Harper & Row, 1972), p. 2.
3. For a classic discussion of utopia, see Karl Mannheim, *Ideology and Utopia: An Introduction to the Sociology of Knowledge* (New York: Harcourt, Brace, Jovanovich, 1955).
4. Ezra Stotland, *The Psychology of Hope* (San Francisco: Jossey-Bass, 1969), p. 5.
5. Gustavo Gutiérrez, *A Theology of Liberation* (Maryknoll, N.Y.: Orbis, 1973), pp. 232-234.
6. This understanding of revelation is in keeping with the tradition that views reason and nature as gracious and grace-full gifts of God that enable us partially to know and understand the truth about God and ourselves. In this way of thinking, revelation completes reason, nature, and experience. Indeed, these are among the central instrumentalities of revelation. The Protestant orthodox and neo-orthodox emphasis upon total depravity insists that revelation is totally contrary to and separate from our experience and capacity for knowledge. Hence, it breaks in upon us as an intrusion from a reality that is totally different from and discontinuous with us.
7. Harold Rugg, *Imagination* (New York: Harper & Row, 1963).
8. See Walter Wink, *The Bible in Human Transformation: Towards a New Paradigm for Bible Study* (Philadelphia: Fortress, 1980).

Chapter 6: "Crucified, Dead, and Buried"

1. Van Leeuwen, *Christianity in World History*, p. 51.
2. Norman K. Gottwald, *The Tribes of Yahweh: A Sociology of the Religion of Liberated Israel, 1250–1050 B.C.* (Maryknoll, N.Y.: Orbis, 1979).
3. Jürgen Moltmann, *A Theology of Hope* (New York: Harper & Row, 1976), p. 129.
4. Gerhard von Rad, *Old Testament Theology*, vol. 2 (New York: Harper & Row, 1967), p. 118.
5. Eugen Rosenstock-Huessy, *The Christian Future* (New York: Harper & Row, 1966), p. 83.
6. Ibid., p. 32.
7. Karl Marx, "Theses on Feuerbach," in *The German Ideology* (New York: International Pub., 1947), Eleventh Thesis.
8. Elie Wiesel, *Night* (New York: Bantam Books, 1982), pp. 59, 60.
9. Ibid., pp. 61, 62.
10. Richard Shaull, *Heralds of a New Reformation* (Maryknoll, N.Y.: Orbis, 1984), p. 24.
11. Quoted in ibid., p. 25

Chapter 7: "New Wineskins for New Wine"

1. H. Richard Niebuhr, *Christ and Culture* (New York: Harper & Row, 1951), pp. 72, 73.
2. Alves, *Tomorrow's Child,*, p. 201.
3. Rubem Alves, *What Is Religion?* (Maryknoll, N.Y.: Orbis, 1984).
4. Alves, *Tomorrow's Child*, p. 197.
5. H. Richard Niebuhr, *Social Sources of Denominationalism* (New York: World, 1972), p. 32.
6. Rosemary Ruether, *The Radical Kingdom* (New York: Harper & Row, 1970), p. 13.
7. For a fuller treatment of this period see Michael Walzer, *The Revolution of the Saints* (Cambridge: Harvard University Press, 1965).
8. Ibid., p. 221.
9. Ibid., p. 225.
10. Gutiérrez, *A Theology of Liberation*, p. 250.
11. Niebuhr, *Social Sources of Denominationalism*, p. 20.
12. Shaull, *Heralds of a New Reformation*, p. 124.
13. Ibid., p. 125.
14. Ibid., p. 126.
15. Sergio Torres and John Eagleson, eds. *The Challenge of Basic Christian Communities* (Maryknoll, N.Y.: Orbis, 1981), p. 191.

Epilogue: "Thy Kingdom Come"

1. George Pixley, *God's Kingdom* (Maryknoll, N.Y.: Orbis, 1981), p. 2.
2. Ibid., p. 100.
3. Ibid., p. 8.

4. Quoted in José Míguez Bonino, *Doing Theology in a Revolutionary Situation* (Philadelphia: Fortress Press, 1975), p. 68.

5. Dietrich Bonhoeffer, *Ethics* (New York: Macmillan, 1949), p. 317.

6. See Cornel West, *Prophesy Deliverance: An Afro-American Revolutionary Christianity* (Philadelphia: Westminster Press, 1982), chapter 3. West discusses the humanist tradition within the Afro-American culture and develops the relationship between what he calls individuality and democracy.

Also by T. Richard Snyder

DIVIDED WE FALL

Moving From Suspicion to Solidarity

*published by
Westminster/John Knox Press
Louisville, Kentucky*

The author offers a theological and ethical guide for people who need each other but frequently are at each other's throats.

"Snyder is dealing with Christian unity in a fresh way. Books on "unity" don't usually grab people, but this one will, both because of its fresh (and somewhat controversial) thesis and because of the clarity of exposition. He is able to use some third world themes in ways that make them alive and applicable to the northern hemisphere."

Robert McAfee Brown

"This is an important note that needs to be heard. Snyder provides a role model for others... (he) provides resources for a wide group of persons asking what they can do with their white, middle-class guilt. Good for white males in the church who are seeking advice on how to move into coalitions (and) good in feminist courses because of its emphasis on men's liberation."

Letty M. Russell

"In this book Snyder continues to grapple with the Biblical meaning of alienation, but here he spells it out more realistically in terms of group differences and divisions, and tries to resolve the problem through interdependence and solidarity in suffering and struggle.

We must listen to the appeal that he is making if the historical project that liberation theology presumes to represent is to be a faithful and effective prescription for the sickness of this world at the turn of the twentieth century."

Gayraud Wilmore

With a study guide to help Christians in their quest for justice and liberation

Available from your Cokesbury Bookstore